Politics

IN AMERICA

OPPOSING VIEWPOINTS®

Other Books of Related Interest in the Opposing
Viewpoints Series:

American Foreign Policy
American Government
American Values
America's Children
America's Defense
America's Elections
America's Future
Censorship
Civil Liberties
Economics in America
The Mass Media
The New World Order
Social Justice
Trade

Politics

IN AMERICA

OPPOSING VIEWPOINTS®

David L. Bender & Bruno Leone, *Series Editors*

Stacey L. Tipp, *Book Editor*
Carol Wekesser, *Book Editor*

OPPOSING VIEWPOINTS SERIES ®

Greenhaven Press, Inc.   PO Box 289009   San Diego, CA 92198-0009

Library of Congress Cataloging-in-Publication Data

Politics in America : opposing viewpoints / Carol Wekesser, book editor. Stacey L. Tipp, book editor.
    p.   cm. — (Opposing viewpoints series)
    Includes bibliographical references and index.
    ISBN 0-89908-189-4 (lib. bdg. : alk. paper)   . — ISBN 0-89908-164-9 (pbk. : alk. paper)
    1. Political parties—United States.   I. Wekesser, Carol, 1963- . II. Tipp, Stacey L., 1963- . III. Series: Opposing viewpoints series (Unnumbered)
JK1726.P65   1992   91-42803
320.973—dc20

92424

"Congress shall make no law . . .
abridging the freedom of speech,
or of the press."

First Amendment to the U.S. Constitution

The basic foundation of our democracy is the first amendment guarantee of freedom of expression. The Opposing Viewpoints Series is dedicated to the concept of this basic freedom and the idea that it is more important to practice it than to enshrine it.

Contents

Why Consider Opposing Viewpoints?

"It is better to debate a question without settling it than to settle a question without debating it."

Joseph Joubert (1754-1824)

The Importance of Examining Opposing Viewpoints

The purpose of the Opposing Viewpoints Series, and this book in particular, is to present balanced, and often difficult to find, opposing points of view on complex and sensitive issues.

Probably the best way to become informed is to analyze the positions of those who are regarded as experts and well studied on issues. It is important to consider every variety of opinion in an attempt to determine the truth. Opinions from the mainstream of society should be examined. But also important are opinions that are considered radical, reactionary, or minority as well as those stigmatized by some other uncomplimentary label. An important lesson of history is the eventual acceptance of many unpopular and even despised opinions. The ideas of Socrates, Jesus, and Galileo are good examples of this.

Readers will approach this book with their own opinions on the issues debated within it. However, to have a good grasp of one's own viewpoint, it is necessary to understand the arguments of those with whom one disagrees. It can be said that those who do not completely understand their adversary's point of view do not fully understand their own.

A persuasive case for considering opposing viewpoints has been presented by John Stuart Mill in his work *On Liberty.* When examining controversial issues it may be helpful to reflect on this suggestion:

The only way in which a human being can make some approach to knowing the whole of a subject, is by hearing what can be said about it by persons of every variety of opinion, and studying all modes in which it can be looked at by every character of mind. No wise man ever acquired his wisdom in any mode but this.

Analyzing Sources of Information

The Opposing Viewpoints Series includes diverse materials taken from magazines, journals, books, and newspapers, as well as statements and position papers from a wide range of individuals, organizations, and governments. This broad spectrum of sources helps to develop patterns of thinking which are open to the consideration of a variety of opinions.

Pitfalls to Avoid

A pitfall to avoid in considering opposing points of view is that of regarding one's own opinion as being common sense and the most rational stance, and the point of view of others as being only opinion and naturally wrong. It may be that another's opinion is correct and one's own is in error.

Another pitfall to avoid is that of closing one's mind to the opinions of those with whom one disagrees. The best way to approach a dialogue is to make one's primary purpose that of understanding the mind and arguments of the other person and not that of enlightening him or her with one's own solutions. More can be learned by listening than speaking.

It is my hope that after reading this book the reader will have a deeper understanding of the issues debated and will appreciate the complexity of even seemingly simple issues on which good and honest people disagree. This awareness is particularly important in a democratic society such as ours where people enter into public debate to determine the common good. Those with whom one disagrees should not necessarily be regarded as enemies, but perhaps simply as people who suggest different paths to a common goal.

Developing Basic Reading and Thinking Skills

In this book, carefully edited opposing viewpoints are purposely placed back to back to create a running debate; each viewpoint is preceded by a short quotation that best expresses the author's main argument. This format instantly plunges the reader into the midst of a controversial issue and greatly aids that reader in mastering the basic skill of recognizing an author's point of view.

A number of basic skills for critical thinking are practiced in the activities that appear throughout the books in the series. Some of the skills are:

Evaluating Sources of Information. The ability to choose from among alternative sources the most reliable and accurate source in relation to a given subject.

Separating Fact from Opinion. The ability to make the basic distinction between factual statements (those that can be demonstrated or verified empirically) and statements of opinion (those that are beliefs or attitudes that cannot be proved).

Identifying Stereotypes. The ability to identify oversimplified, exaggerated descriptions (favorable or unfavorable) about people and insulting statements about racial, religious, or national groups, based upon misinformation or lack of information.

Recognizing Ethnocentrism. The ability to recognize attitudes or opinions that express the view that one's own race, culture, or group is inherently superior, or those attitudes that judge another culture or group in terms of one's own.

It is important to consider opposing viewpoints and equally important to be able to critically analyze those viewpoints. The activities in this book are designed to help the reader master these thinking skills. Statements are taken from the book's viewpoints and the reader is asked to analyze them. This technique aids the reader in developing skills that not only can be applied to the viewpoints in this book, but also to situations where opinionated spokespersons comment on controversial issues. Although the activities are helpful to the solitary reader, they are most useful when the reader can benefit from the interaction of group discussion.

Using this book and others in the series should help readers develop basic reading and thinking skills. These skills should improve the reader's ability to understand what is read. Readers should be better able to separate fact from opinion, substance from rhetoric, and become better consumers of information in our media-centered culture.

This volume of the Opposing Viewpoints Series does not advocate a particular point of view. Quite the contrary! The very nature of the book leaves it to the reader to formulate the opinions he or she finds most suitable. My purpose as publisher is to see that this is made possible by offering a wide range of viewpoints that are fairly presented.

David L. Bender
Publisher

11

Introduction

"Americans view politics with boredom and detachment. For most of us, politics is increasingly abstract, a spectator sport barely worth watching."

E.J. Dionne Jr.,
Why Americans Hate Politics, 1991.

Evidence shows that Americans are apathetic about politics. Voting records reveal that two-thirds of America's citizens who are eligible to vote do not. Political party records indicate that active party membership is seriously declining. The consensus of political analysts is that for the last thirty years, Americans have increasingly felt detached from politics and government. By and large, Americans believe that they have no influence on government policy, that political parties no longer represent their interests, and that voting is ineffective and meaningless.

Experts cite several causes for the increase in apathy and decrease in the public's influence on government. Business consultant Arnold Brown points to the increasing complexity of American society as one factor: "Many Americans keenly feel [a] loss of influence. The size of the United States and the increasing complexity and greater number of critical issues it faces have almost forced this decline in the influence of the public on policy." Brown believes that as issues become more complex, it becomes more difficult for individual constituents to understand and influence government policy. When voters are faced with a complex issue such as the impact of environmental measures on the economy, they are overwhelmed with conflicting information and consequently feel incapable of making good decisions. This feeling of inadequacy and helplessness causes many Americans to avoid the polls altogether. As Brown explains, "This decline in participation is often referred to as 'public apathy,' [but] it is clearly an expression of public frustration and a sense of futility."

As public participation in the voting process declined, the phenomenon of special interest groups began to emerge. These groups, such as the National Organization for Women, the National Right to Life Committee, and the Sierra Club, address

12

only a few issues, such as women's rights, abortion, or the environment. Consequently, their goals are clear and simple to understand. Because these groups can pool all of their resources—money, time, lobbyists, volunteers—behind one issue, such groups are highly effective in pressuring politicians and gaining support. These groups offer Americans who eagerly seek a respite from the complexity of issues a seemingly simple solution. By joining a special interest group that concentrates on one political issue, the average American can regain the sense that he or she can influence government policy at least on some issues facing the nation.

Although special interest groups argue that they provide an opportunity for political action, many critics argue that the groups are more self-serving than beneficial. Each special interest group appeals to a minority of citizens. Special interest groups may also misrepresent public opinion in politics, making it seem as though there is widespread agreement where, in fact, little exists. E.J. Dionne Jr., the author of *Why Americans Hate Politics*, points to the abortion issue as an example:

> Abortion is a morally complex and personally wrenching issue. It is a difficult issue to straddle or compromise. Yet the evidence from polls is that even on this question, Americans resist 'yes/no' answers. The polls show that Americans overwhelmingly believe that abortion should be available in the 'hard' cases, involving rape, incest, or danger to a mother's life. The polls show that Americans are uneasy with government restrictions on abortion in other cases, too, believing it a 'private' matter. Yet the same surveys show that Americans are uncomfortable with how many abortions are being performed and feel that women often resort to abortion in circumstances where they should avoid it.

As Dionne explains, abortion, like many political issues, is complex. But political debate on the issue overlooks this fact and has been dominated by special interest groups who present views that are at odds with what the majority of Americans believe. There is no special interest group for this majority—they have been left out of the political debate, as has the complexity of the issue. The complexity of many political issues is often sacrificed when Americans rely on special interest groups to determine government policy.

What is the answer, then, if special interest groups offer an imperfect solution, political parties no longer seem to represent the majority of Americans, and voting on the issues has become complex and difficult? Whether the voting public can be reinvigorated to take a larger part in the nation's democracy is yet to be seen. The contributors in *Politics in America: Opposing Viewpoints* analyze the reasons for Americans' growing apathy toward politics and offer possible solutions. The book includes the following chapters: Does American Political Leadership Need Improvement? How Can Voter Participation Be Increased? What Political Ideologies Are Important in the U.S.? Does the Two-Party System Effectively Represent Americans? Through the viewpoints presented in the book, the reader will gain a better understanding of America's political process and the relationship between government, politicians, and the people.

Does American Political Leadership Need Improvement?

Chapter Preface

"It is time for a new generation of leadership, to cope with new problems and new opportunities. For there is a new world to be won."—John F. Kennedy, July 4, 1960.

Although John F. Kennedy made the above statement more than three decades ago, his words hold much truth for today's world. Recent momentous changes—the end of the cold war, the political changes in Eastern Europe and the Soviet republics, and the potential for peace in the Middle East, just to mention a few—have led politicians and scholars to label this era the New World Order. In this era, political and economic relationships between nations may change dramatically, bringing new problems and new opportunities to the United States and the world. It is thought that this new era will also require new leaders with a fresh vision. This seems especially true for the foreign policy of the United States, many commentators argue. Because of the demise of the Soviet Union, the United States now stands alone as the preeminent superpower and therefore has a special responsibility to provide leadership.

Yet many Americans question whether the nation's current political leaders are capable of ushering the nation and the world into this new era. A 1989 Gallup poll revealed that fewer than 35 percent of Americans have "a great deal" or "quite a lot" of confidence in their congressional leaders. The words of Auburn University philosophy professor Tibor R. Machan sum up the feelings of many Americans: "Wouldn't it be refreshing to have a candidate who is really concerned about this country's overall solvency and credibility? One might be able to vote for someone like that and feel proud. I am afraid, however, that . . . little is going to change with our present team of leaders." This lack of confidence applies both to foreign policy issues and to domestic issues such as the deficit and unemployment, which many Americans feel have been neglected by politicians.

While Americans have always felt free to express their opinions concerning politicians, the continuing decline in voter turnout and political participation has led some to believe that the dissatisfaction Americans feel today for their leaders is greater than ever. The authors in the following chapter discuss their views concerning the state of American political leadership and make proposals to improve its quality.

"There is nothing wrong with our democratic institutions; there is something wrong with the people within them."

America Is Facing a Leadership Crisis

Lee Brandenburg with Andrew Lewis Shepherd

Lee Brandenburg and Andrew Lewis Shepherd are the authors of *The Captive American*, from which this viewpoint is excerpted. *The Captive American* is a stinging indictment of America's leaders who are, according to Brandenburg and Shepherd, more interested in getting reelected than in governing the country. Career-minded politicians are ruining America, the authors argue, through their neglect of important issues and their relentless pursuit of power and prestige. Brandenburg is a millionaire realtor and a film producer. Shepherd is a political scientist who has worked on political campaigns and has been a Pentagon consultant on U.S.-Soviet relations.

As you read, consider the following questions:

1. According to the authors, what does Michael Deaver's ascent to power tell us about the quality of America's leaders?
2. What do Brandenburg and Shepherd mean by "the scandal inside the Beltway?"
3. How do the authors explain the fact that Americans are dissatisfied with their leaders but continue to reelect them?

Excerpted, with permission, from *The Captive American: How to Stop Being a Political Prisoner in Your Own Country* by Lee Brandenburg with Andrew Lewis Shepherd, Hampton Books, 1988.

In the last year of the Reagan presidency, a year of great political uncertainty and turmoil, Americans became briefly obsessed—and amused—by a scandal involving astrology. The astrology disclosure helped sell hundreds of thousands of copies of an otherwise dull, self-serving book by former White House staffer Donald Regan. I was among the amused. I was also furious.

What do you suppose historians will conclude about America in the 1980s, when they discover that our national decisions were influenced by image-makers and star-gazers at the elbow of the President? What will they think of our politics, our judgment, our taste in books?

The politics of our time have produced a ton of kiss-and-tell books. It's not new; we got the same thing after Watergate, from H.R. Haldeman, Gordon Liddy, Charles Colson and John Dean. Even Nixon keeps writing. What I find disquieting, and so should you, is the deeper meaning of these books. Only in America is failure rewarded twice.

First we pay these people to go to Washington, abuse their power, bungle their jobs and complicate our lives. Then we let them sell their mistakes back to us as history.

The Road to Washington

Have you ever wondered how certain individuals wind up in the seat of power, deciding issues that hit us right in the stomach? I have some insight into one such ascent.

In 1961, I was a recent graduate of San Jose State, and had also recently moved up from real estate broker to land developer in the Santa Clara Valley. Sometimes I would revisit my old campus haunts, including one cocktail lounge in particular, the Interlude.

The piano player there developed a small following. He was another State alumnus, who had belonged to the fraternity next to mine. His name was Mike Deaver.

One night the piano player didn't show up. Turns out Deaver had lost his daytime job.

I learned the rest of the story from one of his frat brothers. Deaver had been accepted by IBM for a six-month training program (people were just beginning to call the area Silicon Valley). One condition of the job was no part-time employment. One night, during the probationary period, his supervisor at IBM happened to walk into the Interlude and caught Mike at the keyboard.

With a career at IBM down the tubes, he studied his options. There was no real job in sight, and the prospect of playing the lounge circuit did not appeal to him. So he settled for politics. I heard that he went to work for the Republican party in Santa Clara County, made connections in Sacramento and wound up on the staff of the new governor of California, Ronald Reagan. From time to time, I would notice his name or picture in the papers. Then I saw he became special assistant to the President, at the pinnacle of the American government. As far as anyone could tell, he made it without ever holding a real job.

I was amused when I saw in his autobiography that Deaver said he went into politics "after I went to work for IBM in sales and concluded that the corporate world was not for me."

The Reagans came to depend on him so fully after 20 years that Deaver was asked to select a gravesite for the couple—and to ask one of Reagan's wealthy supporters to pay for it.

In his later activities as a lobbyist, Deaver joined the list of more than 100 Reagan appointees to be accused of misconduct. Our politicians are really building a legacy for us. No one can say the words "public servant" anymore without laughing. Today a statesman is just a politician who has gray hair and is not presently under indictment.

Who's to Blame?

Remember that we don't have a pure "democracy" where the people decide everything themselves. We're not like Switzerland, with referendums on almost every decision that needs to be made.

As a representative democracy, we elect a small number of our fellow citizens to go to Washington (or the state capital or city hall) and make the day-to-day decisions for us. The people we elect are our "leaders." They form our government—and we expect them to have goals, strategies to achieve them and the ability to rally the public around those goals and strategies.

Good leaders tell the people, as John F. Kennedy did, "ask what you can do for your country." Instead, today's politicians take an easier route, telling people fairy tales and avoiding any hint of hard work or self-sacrifice for the common good. Instead of leaders who might place demands on us, we have "leaders" like Jack Kemp, who appeals to the selfishness in young Americans by saying that "at the age of 18, you should be focusing on your dreams and ambitions, not picking up cans in Yellowstone." These modern politicians like things that way. They're most comfortable when a majority of us don't vote or pay attention to public affairs, leaving the field open to those voters under party control. They want people to "focus on their dreams and ambitions" and ignore what goes on in Washington.

The Scandal Inside the Beltway

The Beltway is Interstate 495, which encircles the District of Columbia, and the city inside is the scandal.

At first glance, Washington is a place where thousands of public servants do their jobs honestly and according to the rules.

But those workers, buried in massive bureaucracies, are hostage to the same political forces as the rest of us. They have little authority of their own, and their good work is often undermined by the abuses of those who do.

The deeper truth is that Washington has become the heart of American political decay. It is a city where a permanent elite holds sway, politicians and their accomplices controlling the money, prestige and power that political supremacy can bring.

There are two groups in our democracy: those who have power, and those who don't. "They" have power, and they have a lock on it. "We" are powerless, partly by default, and we apparently don't care. If we did care, we would use the means available to us to vote the villains out. But half of us don't even vote. The fact is, we have abandoned the principle of accountability that the Founding Fathers laid down as a guiding principle of our democracy.

"Leaders? Sorry, we don't have any leaders. You might try Russia; they seem to have a few."

The average American gives little thought to the philosophy of government we enjoy; for years I never really appreciated the importance of the tenets of democracy. But the straits we are now in make me look back to the efforts made by concerned individuals in another time of American political crisis: the authors of the Constitution.

Wary of an all-powerful state, the Founding Fathers wisely established a government of laws, not men. They were suspicious of centralized, long-held power, and they had no truck with career public "servants." They did everything they could to limit the power that any politician or government bureaucracy could exercise over the American people.

For fights within the government—say, a battle between the executive and the legislative branches over particular functions—the Founding Fathers devised a separation of powers and a system of checks and balances that still holds today. And for the never-ending battle between "us" and "them," the people and the politicians, they built in democratic elections as the ultimate accountability.

In the early days of this country, politicians were on a short leash. When election day came around, the people could yank power-hungry politicians out of Washington before they became entrenched. But in contemporary politics that leash has stretched and weakened, and the natural suspicion that most of us feel about politicians is only getting worse. We feel powerless and betrayed.

The Politics of Distrust

As long ago as 1869, Mark Twain wrote, "I always did hate politics." A century later, John Wayne, in his crusty seventies, summed up the feelings of many Americans when he told a reporter:

I hate politics. I regard it as a necessary evil, a citizen's responsibility. There's no way, even if you went back to the days of the Inquisition, that you could get me to run for political office. Politics in the old days was fun. But now it's become an awesome monster and is apt to ruin the country. Politicians don't do what's good for the country. They do what helps them get elected. I just can't get enthused about politics anymore. I've got to keep making a living.

Wayne's words sound very much like the criticisms that another old actor, Ronald Reagan, used to make of politics. But is it politics we find so ugly or is it the *politicians* we really can't stand? We like "politics" when it enables us to fight for and achieve the policies we believe in or when it delivers the benefits we need—that government check in the mail, for example. We despise the "politicians" for the things they get away with, their blatant self-interest and the perks they enjoy at our expense.

It didn't surprise me to find out that Americans have always looked down on politicians, for the same reasons we do today. Mark Twain zeroed in on the target, saying he was "disgusted with the prevailing political methods, the low ambitions and ideals, of the politicians; dishonesty in office; corruption, and frank distribution of appointments among characterless and incompetent men as pay for party service; the evasion and sometimes straight-out violation of the civil-service laws. . . ."

21

Twain might just as well be writing today. The corruption may not be as blatant—the subtle perks of power have replaced the brown envelope stuffed with cash—but we have always had incompetent and corrupt politicians. Now we just can't seem to get rid of them.

Elected for Life—or Longer

There is nothing wrong with our democratic institutions; there is something wrong with the people within them. The key feature of contemporary politics is something we have never had before in America: a class of *Lifetime Politicians*. Once they get into office, it is nearly impossible to remove them.

Elected Politicians Pursue Their Own Agendas

Life in Washington promotes the self-image of the elected politician. It is comfortable and is fun. It carries with it good pay and attractive privileges, but more than that: it brings power, influence, publicity, fame, and celebrity status. . . .

The nation's politicians are all working hard doing things in pursuit of their private and personal agendas, and find electoral apathy very convenient.

Washington, D.C., as the nation's capital, ought to be filled with people working to serve the common good of the nation. The stark and unpleasant reality is that it is dominated by people passionately driven *to be served*—viewing themselves as being that important. This is the prevailing ethos.

R.V. Raehn, *Conservative Review*, June 1990.

The problem is most obvious in our biggest political fraternity, the U.S. House of Representatives. From 1956 to 1980, incumbents in the House who sought reelection held their seats 92 percent of the time. In the 1982 elections, the percentage of incumbents returned to Congress was 95 percent. In other words, only 5 percent of incumbent representatives actually lost their jobs to an opponent.

In the House elections in 1986, that high return rose to *98 percent*. Out of 435 total incumbents, 393 ran for reelection (the rest had either died or were retiring). Only 8 of 393 went down to defeat.

Let those numbers sink in. In 1986—with all the ills in the economy, our foreign policy debacles, social dislocations—only 2 percent of the incumbents lost re-election. We re-elected the same clowns whose hands were on the rudder as our ship listed toward the shoals! That's not accountability. *That* is the scandal inside the Beltway! . . .

It wasn't always this way. I repeat: *IT WASN'T ALWAYS THIS WAY*. Modern pols are engaged in a careerist pattern which would have been viewed as very peculiar, even un-American, in earlier days. From the start of the Republic right through the 19th century, most Representatives served only *one* term. Turnover at each election averaged around 45 percent, often ranging up to 60 percent. When our great-grandfathers said, "Throw the rascals out," they did it.

Did you know that, before the turn of this century, only a handful of men had made a career of Congress, and they were often ridiculed? The founders intended our system to work that way, with average citizens taking their turns serving in Congress, then returning to their real jobs. In the 19th century, Congress was a part-time body.

Two changes occurred in the first half of the 20th century, one in Congress and one in the way we thought of it. First, Representatives grew more and more frustrated at the ability of the Speaker of the House to appoint committee members and chairmen arbitrarily. In the 1800s high turnover meant "seniority" didn't count for much, so Speakers had a free hand with appointments.

In 1911 new and returning members of Congress revolted and took away the Speaker's powers of appointment, instead installing the seniority system. They wanted to feel they had earned their seats on committees, and the change gave them an incentive to run for reelection . . . and keep running.

The other change came a few decades later, in response to the societal upheavals of the 1930s and 1940s. The New Deal era was a trying time for the country. People everywhere felt overwhelmed by the enormity of the Great Depression, and then by the dark days of World War II. Americans needed to rely on Washington's ability to handle our problems, and they wanted continuity in government. While they were electing Franklin D. Roosevelt to an unprecedented four terms in office, they began to reelect Senators and Representatives to third terms, fourth terms, fifth terms. . . .

Incumbents in the Senate

In 1986, with 34 Senate seats up for grabs, 21 incumbents won reelection while only seven lost. When you add in the winners in states where incumbents had died or retired, the Senate welcomed only 13 new faces that year. (And of course we gave Ronald Reagan another four years in 1984.) Today's politicians would be bewildered if we forced them out of the halls of the House and Senate into real jobs.

How can we expect fresh and innovative thinking in that kind of system? My local Representative, Don Edwards, is a wonder-

23

ful guy, but 25 years have passed since he first went to Congress! The Tenth District is now just another safe seat, so safe that the Republicans couldn't even persuade anyone to challenge Edwards (a Democrat) in 1988.

The syndrome reaches down to lower levels, too. *California* magazine reported that in the 1986 election, every single incumbent who ran for reelection to our state legislature was victorious. The magazine concluded, "There's a dirty little secret of congressional politics in California: hardly anyone loses anymore."

What on earth is going on? To hear the politicians tell it, we simply keep endorsing their work. A local incumbent explained to the *San Jose Mercury News* that voters "think we're doing a marvelous job."

But you and I know that's not why they get reelected. Incumbents are simply better at running for office than they are at running the government. . . .

You might ask what difference it makes to average citizens that they get perpetual incumbents. I'll tell you. Politicians who focus on reelection have little time to deal with issues; great campaigners make lousy leaders. And their experience as incumbents isn't as valuable as they'd like us to believe. In fact, perpetual incumbents see most problems through the lens of their ultimate concern: staying in office.

"Public spirit, even in Congress, lives. "

America Is Not Facing a Leadership Crisis

Steven Kelman

Steven Kelman is the author of *Making Public Policy: A Hopeful View of American Government*, from which this viewpoint is excerpted. In it, Kelman argues that the U.S. government works because there is an abundance of public-spirited individuals in government. In the following viewpoint, which focuses on Congress, Kelman contends that senators and representatives are more interested in creating good public policy and attending to the nation's problems than in seeking their own reelection. Kelman is a professor of public policy and government at Harvard University in Cambridge, Massachusetts.

As you read, consider the following questions:

1. According to Kelman, why do so many people believe that members of Congress are interested only in getting reelected?
2. What features of Congress promote public spirit, according to the author?
3. Who do you find more convincing, Kelman or Brandenburg and Shepherd, the authors of the previous viewpoint? Why?

Among the institutions involved in the political process, Congress, according to the common view, is the one least likely to examine policy alternatives in terms of what would be good for the nation as a whole. Congressmen, it is noted, represent constituencies considerably smaller than the entire country. The exigencies of getting reelected, it is argued, drive them to ask which policy would be in the interests of their constituents, not which would be best for the nation as a whole. (Some would defend this as a matter of conscious institutional design, intended to provide a localistic component in the political process.) A local orientation may be strengthened further because jobs that foster such an orientation attract people who already find it congenial: Samuel Huntington presents interesting statistics showing that the proportion of congressional leaders still living in their hometown is much higher than that of executive branch leaders or corporate executives. Furthermore, the devolution of so much formal authority to committees means that disproportionate power over the results of the process goes to an often unrepresentative subset of the membership as a whole, since members may seek the committee assignments that allow them to shape programs to help their districts. (Members representing rice-growing districts are likely to try to get onto the agriculture subcommittee dealing with price supports for rice.) This also discourages examination of bills from a wider range of considerations. Lack of party discipline may be seen as contributing to the same result, because the process of developing a single position for an entire party encourages a similar broader examination.

A Different Fear

More recently a different fear has been expressed, by journalists more than scholars, of the consequence of the need to return so often to the voters. This is the fear of the effect of campaign contributions and of political action committees on the inclination of representatives to do the right thing. The fear is that political action committees are giving us "the best *Congress money can buy," with members beholden to the interest groups that give them contributions and hence not inclined to examine issues on their merits.

Certainly there is something to all this. Members of Congress naturally care about getting reelected. If nothing else, a natural selection process works to weed out those who do not. To the extent that voters themselves care only about what is best for themselves personally, there will be pressure on congressmen to share that preoccupation. For example, when an issue has a direct effect on a large number of jobs in the district, members can be counted on to vote their constituency rather than to think about what good public policy would be. Antidefense congressmen support weapons systems being built in their districts; free-market congressmen from farm districts support subsidies for the farmers. And the forces that have caused congressmen to rely more on their own efforts for obtaining electoral success increase the tendency of members to seek benefits for their districts or campaign contributions from interest groups.

Anyone who wishes to make even a perfunctory examination could easily find many examples where some or even most members of Congress looked no further than the interest of their district or the demands of some campaign contributors in deciding what stand to take on an issue. Thus it is understandable that Congress can be perceived as dominated by "special interests" or peopled by members who look no further than getting reelected.

Public Spirit in Congress

Nonetheless, many congressmen frequently display public spirit when deciding how to act. A growing body of empirical evidence argues that, when important national issues are at stake, many members vote their ideology—their general conceptions of what kinds of public policies are right—over the interests of their districts. Economist Joseph Kalt, for example, found that the ability to predict a Senator's votes on oil price regulations was significantly improved if one looked at the Senator's overall rating on the liberalism scale of the Americans for Democratic Action in addition to whether the Senator came from an oil-producing or oil-consuming state. For votes on legislation on the environmental regulation of strip mining, overall ideology did a significantly better job in explaining a congressman's vote than did measures of whether the state would gain or lose economically from such legislation. In fact, votes on issues such as child pornography and the neutron bomb, questions totally unrelated to strip mining but tapping an underlying dimension of liberal ideology, did a much better job of predicting votes on strip mining than did the economic interests of the Senator's constituents on the issue.

Evidence of a different sort of public spirit comes from the account of two journalists who spent significant time following Senators Edmund Muskie and John Culver in the late 1970s to observe what the life of a Senator was like. What is especially significant about their accounts is that journalists normally are inclined to expect sleaziness, and yet both these accounts found mostly substance. (Bernard Ashball, who wrote the book on Muskie, was apparently surprised enough by what he saw to title his book, *The Senate Nobody Knows.*) Both volumes are filled with accounts of Senators, mostly in committee settings and hence on issues about which they are knowledgeable, seriously debating the merits of proposed legislation. The accounts of committee mark-up sessions (where committee members craft actual legislative language) on Clean Air Act Amendments, which take up much of the space in Ashball's account, include surprisingly sophisticated arguments about philosophical and practical questions involved in the design of environmental policy.

Other Features of Congress

Those who argue that congressmen pay attention mostly to the particular interests of their constituents or to campaign contributors point to features of Congress as an institution that encourage such behavior. However, there are other features of Congress that promote public spirit.

American Government Does Work

Seen over the broad span of historic time and place, American society works pretty well. We have been spared secret police knocking at our doors; we have enjoyed extended economic prosperity; there has been no widespread starvation. We have absorbed multitudes of the wretched of the earth, succeeded in assuring most people a decent old age, and saved a surprising amount of the natural beauty on the American continent. Compared with our achievements, our problems and shortcomings seem trivial. Although we should not give government all the credit for this, we should not deny it *any* credit either.

Steven Kelman, *Making Public Policy*, 1987.

First, the view that there is a conflict between voting the district and looking at a broader range of concerns assumes that the voters want their representatives to do only the former and will punish them electorally if they do not. Yet if this were so, why would candidates running for election stress so often their independence and their desire to stand up to do what is right? In fact, Americans are split on the question of whether congressmen should vote their own best judgment or the opinion of the majority in the district. Results of the few surveys where citizens have been asked how they believed congressmen should behave in instances of such a conflict show that, depending on the wording, anywhere from one-third to somewhat more than half of the population believes that in such cases representatives should vote their own judgment. These answers suggest that many voters do not necessarily prefer that their representative simply vote the district.

A second feature that encourages public spirit is the growing importance of staff. Staff people tend to be interested in issues and in making an impact on policy. Not having to face election themselves, they are not as concerned as are members of Congress with the district or with campaign contributions (although obviously no wise staffer ignores the concerns of the boss). Like journalists for national media, they tend to regard themselves as representatives for poorly organized groups and as people trying to do the right thing.

Third, as Arthur Maass emphasizes in his book, *Congress and the Common Good,* committee members do not enjoy the unconditional deference of the body as a whole. They must pay attention to whether proposals they are considering are acceptable to the wider range of congressional concerns. Deference to committee proposals can be withdrawn if committees exploit this presumption to advance narrow concerns. Furthermore, the growing practice of multiple committee referral reduces the danger that bills will be considered at the committee stage from only a single, narrow point of view.

Fourth, constituency interests and the interests of campaign contributors may pull in opposite directions. Certainly, lobbyists do attempt to show members how their district would be affected by legislation in which the lobbyists are interested. But the demonstration of commonality between constituency interest and the interests of campaign contributors is frequently difficult or impossible. Competing pressures of this sort can create room for members to exercise independent judgment.

Other Members of Congress

Finally, members of Congress are under the eye not only of their own constituents or of political action committees, but of their colleagues and of the media. Members of Congress spend a great deal of time together and thus can be expected to care about the regard of other congressmen. Furthermore, the more their colleagues respect them, the more influence they are likely to have over floor votes and over the results of legislation. Concern about the regard of their colleagues encourages members to behave so as to gain respect. And the evidence suggests that members tend to respect colleagues who are well informed and able to argue on the merits. The books about both Muskie and Culver emphasize how important the ability to make a credible and convincing argument is as a political asset in Congress. "Real power" in the Senate, Muskie is quoted as saying, "comes from doing your work and knowing what you're talking about. . . . The most important thing in the Senate is credibility." "When a Senator makes a speech," writes Elizabeth Drew in her book on Culver, "he is far more likely to command the attention and respect of his colleagues if he seems to know actually what he is talking about." Along similar lines, a group of

29

freshmen congressmen, discussing their experiences for political scientists, "made frequent allusions to the importance of knowledge and expertise" in determining "who wielded real power in committee and in the House."

A More Accessible Congress

By contrast, it is hard to imagine that ability to advance the interest of a congressman's own constituents would engender much respect among colleagues who do not share the same constituents, except for the kind of respect generally referred to as "grudging." The same is the case for the member who shows special devotion to the interests of some favored lobby or lobbies. And the national media are likely to regard devotion to the mere interests of one's own constituency or of political action committees as a craven bow to "special interests." Since the 1970s there has been an increase in the extent to which the various features of the political process in Congress are public. Previously closed committee mark-up sessions are now public. The number of recorded floor votes has increased. This makes the behavior of members of Congress more accessible to constituents (and, perhaps, especially to lobbyists). But it also makes it more accessible to the media.

Where does this leave us in terms of thinking about the importance of public spirit in animating the behavior of members of Congress? We have adduced features of Congress as an institution that promote attention only to a congressman's constituents or to campaign contributors, and other features that encourage attention to a broader range of considerations. These features, of course, balance differently in the minds of different members. Richard Fenno noted this prosaic truth when he pointed out in his study, *Congressmen in Committees*, that members have different primary goals. Some mainly seek assured reelection; others mainly seek influence within Congress; still others mainly seek to formulate good public policy. Also, these considerations balance out differently for different issues. Although few members vote against their constituency on matters of overriding concern to the district, such bills constitute only a small proportion of those before Congress. Similarly, congressmen try to get discretionary government funds for public works and government buildings in their districts, but this makes up only a modest proportion of the federal budget. "The question of where a few thousand office workers will be located is usually secondary," notes R. Douglas Arnold, "to the issue of exactly what they will do." And lobbyists tend to be most effective on technical, low-visibility issues—although I am sensitive to the observation that the distinction between important issues and technical ones may be similar to the one in the story about the family where one spouse made the "important" decisions about whether we should give aid to Nicaragua and the other the "unimportant" ones about what the family should eat for dinner.

Presidents and Public Spirit

There is much talk of the tendency of the American political system to produce political leaders who are pragmatic to the point of lacking all conviction. For all that talk, most modern presidents—our politicians who have come furthest—have been, if anything, overly stern in their public spirit and too slow to compromise with others. Presidents Truman and Ford vetoed bills with regularity. President Carter's stiff-neckedness brought down an entire administration. In 1985 Ronald Reagan, flush from a landslide election victory and needing every ounce of his political prestige to get difficult budget and tax cuts through Congress, was willing to take it on the chin, for essentially no domestic political reward, to honor a commitment to the chancellor of West Germany to visit a German war cemetery where, it turned out, SS troops were buried.

Steven Kelman, *Making Public Policy*, 1987.

A study that measured the significance of "the district" in explaining the votes of congressmen has found a long-term decline in the influence of constituency interests on voting behavior beginning around the time of the New Deal. It is important to note that the big increases in government spending since the 1950s have not been in federal grants to localities, which provide visible constituency benefits, but rather in various general transfer programs that do not allow members to demonstrate that they have gotten something special for the district. In addition, the tendency since the beginning of the 1970s has been to decrease dramatically the use of categorical grants to localities and to increase the use of formula ones. As R. Douglas Arnold points out, this is exactly the opposite of the prediction that would be generated by a view that members singlemindedly seek reelection by bringing goodies to their districts for which they can claim credit. Localities must *apply* for categorical grants, and members can therefore take credit for helping their districts get them. Formula grants, by contrast, are allocated automatically. They are generally not even tied to specific projects, where congressmen can be present at the opening ceremonies and cut a ribbon. Yet it is the formula grants that are increasing, not the categorical ones. This shift is the result of a debate on the merits of federal versus local control.

A similarly interesting phenomenon has been the occasions in

31

recent years when Congress has voted to *deprive* itself of the opportunity to provide visible constituency benefits, by granting formal authority to the executive branch or by legislating automatic formulas. In trade policy, Congress has given up the opportunity to save constituents in trouble from foreign imports by forswearing tariff power to the executive branch. And when Congress indexed social security benefits in 1972 it denied itself the chance each year to vote politically visible benefit increases. In the Gramm-Rudman budget balancing legislation of 1986 Congress deprived itself of the opportunity to save politically popular programs by requiring certain budget cuts. Each of these three situations shares something in common. If Congress legislated in these areas, there would be intense constituency pressures to act a certain way—to protect threatened industries, to legislate large social security increases, to save popular programs. Yet in each case the policies that would result from such pressures would go against what most congressmen believe to be good public policy—free trade, moderate benefit increases, a balanced budget. So, like the psychopathic murderer who pleads, "Stop me before I kill again," members of Congress have voted to deprive themselves of some things that many commentators believe they seek above all—power and the chance to provide visible constituency benefits—so as to bring about good public policy.

Public Spirit Lives in Congress

One interesting piece of evidence on the relative significance of constituency versus broader considerations in the minds of members is that the most sought-after committees in Congress are not those that dispense benefits to constituents, such as Public Works, or those that help members procure a stable of eager campaign workers, such as Post Office and Civil Service. They are, rather, the committees that deal with broad issues of national policy. Furthermore, in a 1977 survey of members of the House, the most common problem members cited about their work-load pressures was that "constituent demands detract from other functions." The view among congressmen appears to be that they should look after their constituency to make sure to be around to do the important thing—participating in making public policy. Public spirit, even in Congress, lives.

"Term limitation brings good candidates which improves the body politic."

Limiting Terms of Legislators Will Improve American Leadership

Edward H. Crane

Currently, U.S. senators and representatives can be reelected an unlimited number of times. In recent years, some Americans, including the author of the following viewpoint, have demanded that limits be placed on the number of terms legislators can serve. Since unlimited reelection means that legislators can potentially remain in office for many years, Edward H. Crane contends that many of them come to regard politics as a career. Consequently, he continues, they become more interested in remaining in office and advancing their own interests than in governing the country. Crane argues that term limitations will rid the nation of these self-interested career politicians. Crane is president of the Cato Institute, a libertarian public policy research foundation in Washington, D.C.

As you read, consider the following questions:

1. Why has government grown so rapidly since 1950, according to Crane?
2. What are the main advantages to term limitations, according to the author?
3. What does Crane mean by the "culture of ruling"?

Edward H. Crane, "Term Limits for a Citizen Legislature," a speech delivered to the Conference on Term Limits, Unruh Institute of Politics, University of Southern California, Los Angeles, California, October 4, 1990.

33

Let me say at the outset that one of the things that endears me most to the concept of legislative term limitation is the fact that inside the Beltway, where I work in Washington, DC, there are few proposals so wildly unpopular. The media hate the idea. Corporate lobbyists hate it. Unions hate it. Trade associations hate it. And most of all, congressmen hate it.

It is, we are told, a know-nothing proposal that would restrict democracy. It would rob America of its most experienced legislators. Permanent legislative staffs would manipulate naive, inexperienced congressmen and state legislators. Special interests will rape and pillage our society, and if that's not enough, it's rumored that Saddam Hussein is the real author of Prop. 140 [the successful initiative limiting the terms of California's elected officials].

High Public Support

And yet, 70 percent of Americans think it's a great idea. In a sense, term limitation is an issue that crystallizes the crisis in the political economy of modern America. More than two hundred years ago Thomas Jefferson, an outspoken advocate of rotation in office, wrote that "the natural progress of things is for government to gain ground and for liberty to yield." In making that point Jefferson became an early exponent of the Public Choice school of political economy. Later, James Buchanan would get the Nobel Prize for his work in Public Choice theory, but the point of that work remains essentially the same, namely, that democratic government, left unattended by constitutional or legislative constraints, has a tendency to grow regardless of the true desires of the people or the cost that growth imposes on the people.

And it would appear that the constraints we presently have in place are failing to get the job done—that is, if we're to believe polls that show the overwhelming majority of Americans believe government is too big and that legislators, at both the state and federal level, have lost touch with the people. Whether those polls are accurate or not, there is ample evidence that government is indeed getting larger.

140 or so years after the founding of this nation, government spending at all levels—federal, state, and local—amounted to just about 10 percent of national income. By 1950, that figure had risen to 26 percent, and today it stands at a remarkable 43 percent of national income.

And as has been well documented, the growth of the federal government is not the sole culprit here. State and local taxes, as one measure, have grown since 1950 from 6 percent of GNP [gross national product] to nearly 11 percent today.

Now, to be sure, there are many reasons for this growth and

the unlimited terms of out-of-touch legislators is hardly the only one. Some of the growth of government is a function of the real, unprompted, demands of Americans. Some of it comes—and I hope that in this day and age people of all political persuasions will admit this is true—some of it comes from the Public Choice dynamic described by Jim Buchanan and others. That is to say, politicians and bureaucrats don't neatly fit the disinterested public servant model described in high school civics texts. It turns out that they, like the rest of us, have interests of their own and quite often those interests are at odds with the interests of the general public. In government, one's stature, power and income is often and perversely a function of being able to increase costs rather than decrease them.

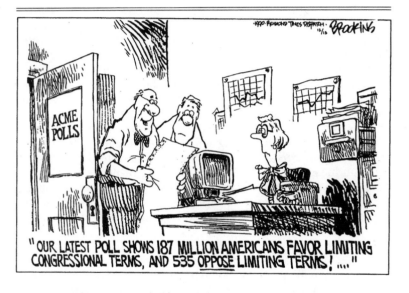

"OUR LATEST POLL SHOWS 187 MILLION AMERICANS FAVOR LIMITING CONGRESSIONAL TERMS, AND 535 OPPOSE LIMITING TERMS! ...."

Gary Brookins © 1990. Reprinted with permission.

Then there is what Milton Friedman and others refer to as the "tyranny of the status quo"—the idea that a program may be debated in Congress for years, decades even, only to eventually pass into law by a single vote. But from that point forward the only debate centers on whether the program's budget should be increased by 5 percent or 15 percent. Whether it has achieved what its backers claimed it would, or whether its budget had perhaps exceeded original projections, are questions polite people in Washington and Sacramento don't ask.

And here the limitless term does have an impact. For logrolling is a very real part of the legislative imperative. You scratch my back and I'll scratch yours. Well, that doesn't just refer to current and proposed legislation. It also applies to past legislation. Without term limitations there will always be members in a given legislature who have been there for twenty or thirty years or longer. They will have sponsored some of these major programs and it will be understood as part of the logrolling process that younger legislators are to keep their hands off.

The Advantages of Limitations

As a result, we either are extraordinarily fortunate that our legislatures never made mistakes, or we continue to suffer, usually on an increasingly expensive basis, for what are very real mistakes. With term limits I don't believe we'd have that problem. With a high turnover and less deadwood in the legislature there would be a much greater willingness to look at past legislation and consider repealing it if it had proven counterproductive to the public interest. Certainly that could have been the case with the S&L crisis which snuck up on us with all the speed of an elderly snail. For years, in the case of my institute, for nearly a decade, people have been predicting a disaster in the savings and loan industry because federal deposit insurance, as constructed, guarantees virtually unlimited deposits what with brokered accounts being wired instantaneously in sums of $100,000 to the S&L with the highest interest rate, regardless of the soundness of that institution's investment portfolio. Depositor discipline has been circumvented and the free market short-circuited. So we have a $500 billion taxpayer bailout in the works courtesy of the "experienced legislators" we might lose if we had term limitation.

This might be a good time for me to define what I'm advocating in the way of term limits, as quite obviously those of us who support term limitation have different approaches. What I would like to see is a return to the Citizen Legislatures envisioned by the founders of this nation who, I believe, would have been appalled at the idea of professional politicians, of professional legislators. How in the world, they would have wondered (and correctly so) can you be a representative of the people if your career job is being a legislator? What I would like to see are legislatures in which the men and women who populate them consider themselves to be, in essence, on a leave of absence from their real job. That means limiting terms in the lower house to six years (as Prop. 140 does) and in the upper house to six or eight years. To me, the beneficial effects of term limitation are in good measure lost when you start talking about twelve years, or especially twelve years, out two, and back in for another twelve. Twelve years is not a leave of absence it's a career-length tenure.

The salutory effects of this "leave of absence," citizen legislature are two-fold. First, and this it seems to me is not insignificant, I believe you would see a more appropriate cross-section of society seeking and obtaining office. The archetype of the law school graduate who becomes a legislative aide for a city councilman straight out of school and works his way up to the state legislature and Congress, would be less prevalent. Instead, we would find more women running, more non-lawyers from the private sector, and more people who simply have the commonsense not to want to spend the rest of their lives running other people's lives. The way it is now, if you want to have serious influence in Congress you had better plan on staying there for fifteen or twenty years. A lot of good people find that an unattractive prospect. So one positive effect a term limitation would be to improve the preselection process of those seeking office in the first place.

Second, and this really gets to the core of why I support term limitation, there is a corrupting process that occurs inside the Beltway in Washington, DC, and in the nation's state capitals. And by "corrupting" I don't mean in the criminal sense (although that clearly enough occurs, as well), but rather in the sense of distorting one's sense of perspective, of disassembling the priority of values one brings from private society. This is not some brilliant insight on my part. It's long been noticed. They even have a name for it in Washington—Potomac Fever. But I think it's an under-appreciated phenomenon.

The Dominant Culture

There is in the legislative centers of America—and, indeed, around the world—what has been called a "culture of spending" but what is really more than that. It is a culture of ruling. A culture quite different from that outside the Beltway. In fact a culture that is mildly disdainful of those outside it. There is, in my view, something unnatural about living in an environment in which virtually everyone is involved in the process of spending other people's money or in regulating other people's lives. This is the environment in which legislators find themselves. And they would be less than human if they weren't influenced by it. They would be less than human if they weren't influenced by the fact that all day long they have microphones in their faces. "What do you think about the budget package, Sen. Dole?" "What are you going to do about the drought, Speaker Brown?"

The longer otherwise decent people stay in legislatures, the more they begin to believe their opinion on everything under the sun is important—much more important than it really is. What's worse, the longer they're there, the stronger is the urge

37

they have to codify in law what they think about everything under the sun. About 1600 laws are passed annually by California's legislators. It is a corrupting process. I've seen it happen time and time again, and it's not just my anecdotal observations. If you look at the voting records of congressmen—and this has been verified by groups ranging from the National Taxpayers Union to the Citizens for a Sound Economy—the longer they are in office, the bigger spenders they become. And this is only logical. As their network of deals, obligations, and reciprocal arrangements expands, so too does the necessity to vote "aye" on spending measures.

The Culture of Ruling

Term limitation would go a long way toward countering the culture of ruling. We're all familiar with the relevant numbers. In the 1960s, according to my colleague Doug Bandow, 142 incumbents were defeated. In the 1970s only 97 went down to defeat, and in the last decade the number fell to just 88 (out of 2175 races). In the 1990 national elections we witnessed the astounding 99 percent reelection rate for U.S. representatives, and of the six who lost, five were under an ethical cloud. In California, there have been 580 state legislative races since 1982 and only nine times has the incumbent been defeated. Worse, in the overwhelming number of cases the incumbents won by a landslide. We can never have Citizen Legislatures under these conditions.

Improved Relations

The American people . . . would like a Congress which, if more "amateurish," nevertheless had less of a stake in the existing system. Above all, they would like a Congress that is in "closer touch" with the people—and nothing can guarantee that more firmly than the certainty that after 12 years, a congressman would return to the "real world." If that's the world he is going to inhabit, he is likely to regard it more respectfully and be less manipulative in his relations with it.

Congress, today, is not in good repute with the American public. A 12-year limitation may be the price we have to pay for reviving its reputation. And, all in all, it may not be much of a price.

Irving Kristol, *American Legion*, February 1991.

The answer doesn't lie in spending limits, in government funding of campaigns, or any other measure that would further rigidify the electoral process. Yes, we can and should limit the perks of incumbency—it is mildly bizarre that congressmen annually send out 12,000 letters for every one they receive from a constituent—but there will always be an inherent advantage to incumbency. Political scientists and other good government types don't like to hear this, but there is a perfectly rational reason for voters to be ignorant of what their congressmen or state legislator is up to. The chance that their vote might make a difference in the election is not worth the cost of studying their legislator's voting record. The truth is, for better or for worse, that these days most voters can't volunteer the name of their own legislators (although they do recognize it in the voting booth), much less expound on the legislation their representatives have sponsored.

Adjusting for gubernatorial and senatorial elections in 1986, the last non-presidential election year, only 27.6 percent of those eligible cast votes for the House of Representatives. Mandated rotation in office through term limitation will at least bring some interest back to election night. Open seats bring competitive elections which bring out the voters. Term limitation brings good candidates which improves the body politic.

"Term limits . . . could deprive the country of the experience and wisdom gained by an incumbent, perhaps just when that experience is needed most."

Term Limitations Would Not Improve American Political Leadership

Charles R. Kesler

Charles R. Kesler is a professor of government at Claremont McKenna College in Claremont, California, and an editor of *Keeping the Tablets: Modern American Conservative Thought.* In the following viewpoint, Kesler opposes limiting the number of terms a senator or representative can serve. He argues that term limits would deprive the country of the wisdom and experience gained by incumbents with long tenure in office. Kesler further believes that if Americans are dissatisfied with their leaders, the appropriate course of action is to vote them out of office, not to limit terms.

As you read, consider the following questions:

1. How did the Federalists and the Anti-Federalists view term limitations, according to Kesler?
2. What does the author believe is responsible for the professionalization of American politics in the twentieth century?

Charles R. Kesler, "Bad Housekeeping: The Case Against Congressional Term Limitations." Reprinted with permission from the Summer 1990 issue of *Policy Review*, the flagship publication of The Heritage Foundation, 214 Massachusetts Ave. NE, Washington, DC 20002.

Everyone complains about Congress, but nobody does anything about it. Frustration with our national legislature, which is by almost every measure widespread among the American public, is about to be exploited by a national movement to throw the rascals out—the rascals, in this case, being incumbent congressmen and senators who have so mastered the art of re-election as to be thought unremovable by conventional means. The most widely touted solution to the problem is the extreme one of adding an amendment to the Constitution limiting the number of terms that members of the House and Senate can serve. . . .

This movement builds on the public's mounting dissatisfaction with a Congress that is seen not only as unresponsive but also as incompetent and corrupt. Indeed, in light of the chronically unbalanced federal budget, Congress's reluctance to perform even its minimal duty of passing a budget (balanced or not) without resort to omnibus continuing resolutions and reconciliation acts, the 51 percent salary increase for its members that it tried to brazen through without a roll call vote, the generous privileges it extends to its members (large staffs, multiple offices, free travel allowances, frequent mailings at public expense, liberal pensions), the corruption-tinged resignations of former House Speaker Jim Wright and former Democratic Whip Tony Coelho, the metastasizing scandal of the Keating Five—in light of all these things, it is a wonder that congressmen get re-elected at all.

And yet that is the paradox. Despite a deep dissatisfaction with Congress as an institution, the American people are re-electing their congressmen (that is, members of the House) at the highest rates in history. In the 1986 and 1988 elections, more than 98 percent of incumbent congressmen seeking re-election were returned to office. By now we have all heard the jokes about there being more turnover in the British House of Lords or in the Soviet Politburo than in the U.S. House of Representatives. The interesting question is, Why? . . .

Anti-Federalists: "Virtue Will Slumber"

This is not the first time in American history that a limit on the reeligibility of elected federal officials has been proposed. At the Constitutional Convention in 1787, whether the president ought to be eligible for reelection was extensively debated, although always in close connection with the related questions of his term of office and mode of election. With the invention of the electoral college and with his term fixed at four years it was thought to be productive of good effects and consistent with his independence from the legislature to allow the president to be eligible for reelection indefinitely; and so it remained until the 22nd Amendment was added to the Constitution. But what is less well known is that the Constitutional Convention also considered limitations on the reeligibility of the lower house of the legislature. The so-called Virginia Plan, introduced by Edmund Randolph, would have rendered members of the House ineligible for reelection for an unspecified period after their term's end. The period was never specified because the Convention expunged the limitation less than a month after it had been proposed.

Nevertheless, the question of limiting congressional terms lived on. It was taken up vigorously by the Anti-Federalists, the opponents of the new Constitution, who urged that "rotation in office" be imposed not so much on House members as on senators, whose small numbers, long term of office, and multifaceted powers made them suspiciously undemocratic. The Anti-Federalists built upon the legacy of the Articles of Confederation, which had required that members of Congress rotate out after serving three one-year terms within any five-year period. . . .

The current appeal for limits on congressional office-holding echoes the major themes of the Anti-Federalists 200 years ago. One of the most rigorous of the Constitution's critics, the writer who styled himself "The Federal Farmer," put it this way: "[I]n a government consisting of but a few members, elected for long periods, and far removed from the observation of the people, but few changes in the ordinary course of elections take place among the members; They become in some measure a fixed body, and often inattentive to the public good, callous, selfish, and the fountain of corruption." After several years in office, he continued, it will be expedient for a man "to return home, mix with the people, and reside some time with them; this will tend to reinstate him in the interests, feelings, and views similar to theirs, and thereby confirm in him essential qualifications of a legislator." Were the people watchful, they could recall him on their own and substitute a new representative at their discretion. But they are not sufficiently vigilant. . . .

Federalists: The People Are Not Fools

The Anti-Federalist arguments were rejected by the advocates of the new Constitution. However, it is only for the presidency that the authors of the most authoritative defense of the Constitution, *The Federalist*, give a detailed refutation of the scheme of rotation in office. In *The Federalist*'s view, there is "an excess of refinement" in the notion of preventing the people from returning to office men who had proved worthy of their confidence. The people are not fools, at least not all of the time, and they can be trusted to keep a reasonably sharp eye on their representatives. So far as history can confirm such a proposition, it seems to pronounce in favor of *The Federalist*. Throughout the 19th and most of the 20th centuries, American politics was not characterized by a professional class of legislators insulated from the fluctuations, much less the deliberate changes, of public opinion. In the 19th century, it was not unusual for a majority of the membership of Congress to serve only one term; congressional turnover consistently averaged 40 to 50 percent every election. Occasionally it reached 60 or 70 percent.

Term Limits Will Make Congress Irrelevant

Limiting terms without other substantive changes would make the federal government less, rather than more, responsive. About 50% of the House and Senate would at all times be filled with trainees, just beginning to learn the ropes. Capitol Hill is already too much the domain of congressional staffers. Limit congressional terms, and staffers alone would be the repositories of institutional memory and the architects of enduring coalitions with the permanent government. . . .

To demand that Congress become the home of short-term amateurs while the rest of the government is the province of long-term professionals is to guarantee the irrelevancy of Congress. For an institution already stricken by what sometimes appears to be terminal gridlock, that would be the final blow.

Hodding Carter III, *The Wall Street Journal*, October 4, 1990.

The young Abraham Lincoln, for example, served only one term in the House of Representatives, in keeping with an informal rotation agreement he had negotiated with two Whig Party rivals in his district. Such agreements were not uncommon, and betokened a vigorous intraparty political life as well as keen competition between the parties: no party wanted its officeholders to betray an unrepublican ambition. But ambition was controlled informally by rotation within a party's bank of candidates so that the party and the country enjoyed the best of both worlds—a circulation of capable and experienced men through public office, with the possibility of keeping truly exceptional ones in office if circumstances demanded it. . . .

The Swing Era Ends

Today's entrenched Congress is a product of the great changes in American politics that have occurred since the late 19th century, particularly the weakening of political parties and the great increase in the size and scope of the federal government. Serving in Congress has become a profession over the past 100 years. The average (continuous) career of congressmen hovered around five years at the turn of the century, already up significantly from its earlier levels; today, the figure has doubled again, with the average member of the House serving about 10 years. In the century after 1860, the proportion of freshmen in the House plummeted from nearly 60 percent to around 10 percent, about where it remains today. This gradual professionalization of Congress owes something to the gradual increase of power in Washington, which made it more attractive to hold office; and still more to the seniority system, introduced in the House after the famous revolt against the power of the Speaker around 1910. With the seniority system in place, districts had great incentives to keep their representatives serving continuously. But the contemporary problems of incumbency are something else again. Since 1971, when House Democrats voted in their caucus to elect committee chairmen by secret ballot rather than follow the rule of committee seniority, the perquisites of seniority have declined, in part. Yet congressional reelection rates have risen. If it is not the advantages of seniority that account for today's almost invulnerable incumbents, then what is it?

The Incumbency Problem

Since the Second World War, reelection rates have been very high, averaging more than 90 percent; they have risen even further recently, approaching 100 percent in the last few elections. The political scientist David Mayhew identified the key to the incumbency problem as "the vanishing marginals," that is, the decline over the past 40 years in the number of marginal or competitive House districts. (A victory margin of 50 to 55 percent makes a district marginal, that is, capable of being won by a challenger.) In 1948 most incumbents won narrowly, getting less than 55 percent of their district's vote. Twenty years later, three-fourths of the incumbents received 60 percent or more of their district's vote, making these essentially safe seats for the winning congressmen. So, not only are more incumbents than ever winning, they are winning by bigger margins than ever before.

Explanations for the decline in marginal districts have not been scarce. First, there is the effect of gerrymandered congressional districts, which tend to be drawn in such a fashion as to lock in incumbents of both parties. Researchers have shown, however, that marginal districts declined just as sharply in the 1960s in states that did *not* redistrict as in those that did; so gerrymandering cannot be the principal culprit. Then there is the effect of incumbency itself—the franking privilege, free publicity stemming from benefits delivered to the district, prodigious sums of money contributed by political action committees, all of which make possible the greater name recognition that is supposed to discourage unknown and underfunded challengers. As the rates of incumbent reelection have climbed, therefore, one would expect an increase in incumbents' name recognition. But, as John Ferejohn

44

and other analysts have shown, the data do not bear this out: incumbents are no better known now than they were before the marginal districts started vanishing. For all of the incumbents' advantages in name recognition, this factor cannot be the crucial one in explaining the decline in competitive House districts.

Faceless Bureaucracy's Friendly Face

In his arresting book *Congress: Keystone of the Washington Establishment,* the political scientist Morris Fiorina puts his finger on the nub of the problem. During the 1960s, congressmen began to put an unprecedented emphasis on casework or constituent service and pork-barrel activities as a way to ensure their reelection. The new emphasis was made possible precisely by "big government," the federal government's expansion of authority over state and local affairs that began dramatically with the New Deal and accelerated during the Great Society. As the federal bureaucracy expanded, more and more citizens found themselves dealing directly with federal agencies—the Social Security Administration, the Veterans Administration, the Equal Employment Opportunity Commission, the Environmental Protection Agency, and so on. To penetrate the mysteries of the administrative state, to find a friendly face amid the "faceless" bureaucrats and a helping hand among so many seemingly determined to do injustice in particular cases, citizens began increasingly to turn to their congressman for succor.

And they were encouraged to do so, particularly by the younger and more vulnerable congressmen who had come into office in the great Democratic waves of 1964 and 1974. Eventually, however, almost all congressmen caught on to the "new deal" made possible and necessary by the increased reach of Washington. The beauty of the new politics was that the same congressmen who were applauded for creating new federal agencies to tackle social problems also got credit for helping their constituents through the labyrinths of these impersonal bureaucracies. In Fiorina's words: "Congressmen take credit coming and going. They are the alpha and the omega." The more ambitious of them exploit the paradox shamelessly: the more bureaucracy they create, the more indispensable they are to their constituents. To which one must add: the longer they've been around Washington, the more plausible is their claim to know precisely how to aid their constituents with the bureaucracy.

It is clear that knowledge of these bureaucratic folkways is more important to voters than ever before. But it requires only a very small number of swing voters, perhaps only 5 percent or so, to transform a district from being marginal or competitive into being safe (thus increasing the incumbent's vote from, say, 53 to 58 percent). To explain the disappearing marginal districts it is therefore necessary only for a very small sector of the electorate to have been won over to the incumbent by the constituent service and pork-barrel opportunities opened up by an activist federal government. To this group of voters in particular, perhaps to most voters to one degree or another, the congressman's job is now thought to be as much administrative as political. The spirit of nonpartisan, expert administration—central to modern liberalism as it was conceived in the Progressive Era—is gradually coloring the public's view of the House of Representatives, transforming it from the most popular branch of the legislature into the highest branch of the civil service. . . .

Term Limits Will Eliminate Good and Bad Legislators

Ultimately, what the term limit amounts to is an indictment of citizenship. It is an admission that the voters are civic imbeciles who cannot discriminate between bad lawmakers and good ones. Where surgical strikes are needed to eliminate the incompetent or corrupt, the term limitation uses carpet bombing in the hope that in the resulting carnage, some of the guilty will suffer along with the innocent.

At the most basic level, term limitation is just flat-out wrongheaded and illogical: To throw everybody out when all you want to do is throw out the rascals is like burning down your house in order to get rid of the rats.

Ross K. Baker, *Los Angeles Times*, October 10, 1990.

Given the origins and nature of the problem with Congress (really with the House of Representatives, inasmuch as Senate incumbents remain beatable), it is apparent that limiting congressional terms to 12 years [the limit suggested by the organization, Americans to Limit Congressional Terms] will do little or nothing to remedy the situation. Any new faces that are brought to Washington as the result of such an amendment will find themselves up against the same old incentives. They will still be eligible for reelection five times. How will they ensure their continued political prosperity without seeing to constituents' administrative needs? If anything, these new congressmen will find themselves confronting bureaucrats rendered more powerful by the representatives' own ignorance of the bureaucracy; for in the administrative state, knowledge is power. It is likely, therefore, that the new congressmen will initially be at a disadvantage relative to the agencies. To counter this they will seek staff members and advisers who are veterans of the Hill, and perhaps larger and more district-oriented staffs to help ward off challengers who would try to take advantage of their inexperience. Is it wise to increase the already expansive power of bureaucrats and congressional staff for the sake of a new congressman in the district every half-generation or so?

The proposed limitation on congressional terms would also have most of the disadvantages of the old schemes of rotation in office that were criticized by the Federalists. Consider these points made by Alexander Hamilton in *Federalist* No. 72 (concerning rotation in the presidency, but still relevant to rotation in Congress). In the first place, setting a limit on office-holding "would be a diminution of the inducements to good behavior. By allowing indefinite reeligibility, political men will be encouraged to make their interest coincide with their duty, and to undertake "extensive and arduous enterprises for the public benefit" because they will be around to reap the consequences. Second, term limits would be a temptation to "sordid views" and "peculation." As Gouverneur Morris put it at the Constitutional Convention, term limits say to the official, "make hay while the sun shines." Nor does a long term of eligibility (12 years in this case) remove the difficulty. No one will know better than the present incumbent how difficult it will be to defeat the future incumbent. So the limits of his career will always be visible to him, as will the temptation to "make hay" as early as possible.

A third disadvantage of term limits is that they could deprive the country of the experience and wisdom gained by an incumbent, perhaps just when that experience is needed most. This is particularly true for senators, whose terms would be limited even though Senate races are frequently quite competitive (recall 1980 and 1986) and that the Senate was precisely the branch of the legislature in which the Framers sought stability, the child of long service. . . .

Congressional term limitations would be at best a distraction. If the American people want to vote all incumbents out of office, or just those particular incumbents known as liberal Democrats, they can do so with but the flick of a lever. All they need is a good reason.

"We should . . . consciously [seek] to draw into politics people of virtue."

Recruiting Individuals with High Moral Standards Would Improve Leadership

Lee H. Hamilton

In the following viewpoint, Lee H. Hamilton argues that Americans are losing faith in their leaders because so many elected representatives have been charged with ethical or legal misconduct in recent years. Hamilton suggests that people of virtue must be recruited to serve in American politics, or public trust in government will erode and the system will ultimately fail. Hamilton, a Democratic congressman from Indiana, chaired the U.S. House of Representatives committee that investigated the Iran-contra affair. This scandal, which rocked the public's confidence in the ethics of the Reagan administration, concerned allegations that the U.S. government provided illegal military aid to the Nicaraguan contras.

As you read, consider the following questions:

1. Why does the author believe Americans are uneasy about morality and ethics in government?
2. How did the deception and dishonesty of the Iran-contra scandal affect public policy, according to Hamilton?

Lee H. Hamilton, "The Need for People of Virtue," *Ethics: Easier Said than Done*, Spring/Summer 1988, vol. 1, pp. 94, 136, 137. Reprinted with permission.

Americans are uneasy about morality and ethics in high places. Unfortunately, there seems to be good cause. At least 21 members of Congress were indicted between 1978 and 1988. Between 1981 and 1988, more than 100 Reagan administration officials were in the news for alleged ethical or legal misconduct—an unprecedented number. . . . Almost every state and major city has confronted a scandal among its public officials. In 1986, the Justice Department obtained more than 1,000 convictions in cases of public corruption. This kind of behavior has led to a broad cynicism—if not ridicule—among Americans. It has made them uneasy about the health of our system of government.

Ethics Questions Are Important

Some say that politicians just reflect a looser moral climate in America, where sexual indiscretions, selfishness, "white lies," and an "enrich-thyself" philosophy—though not praiseworthy—are not that uncommon. Others say that public officials today face stricter standards and tougher scrutiny than in the past. My view is that things are not as they should be and that "ethics questions" are important ones to ask.

While not every action of candidates or public officials should be open for scrutiny, the public does have a legitimate interest in activities which could impair the ability of officeholders to carry out their official duties or which would bring discredit on the institutions of government.

The misconduct of any government official reflects on all government officials, even those who, often under the most difficult circumstances, have conducted themselves according to high ethical and professional standards.

Public leaders face a crisis of confidence. There are significant social costs when the public trust is violated. Opinion polls indicate that a lack of confidence in the integrity of elected officials is a major reason for the low voter turnout in recent elections. Without trust, democratic government just does not work.

Moreover, dishonesty and deception lead to bad policy. That was one of the major lessons of the Iran-contra hearings. During the testimony we heard people claim that the ends justify the means, and that lying to Congress and to the American people is an acceptable practice.

Such attitudes almost guarantee policy failure. Lying and deception about our sale of arms to Iran led to confusion and disarray at the highest levels of government, undermined our credibility with our key allies, and harmed President Reagan's ability to gain and sustain congressional and public support for his policies.

So often during the hearings I was reminded of President Jef-

49

ferson's statement: "The whole art of government consists in the art of being honest."

Our Founding Fathers recognized that no matter how well-structured government is, it will not work unless its offices are held by people of virtue. Public officials, they said, should possess a "disinterested attachment to the public good, exclusive and independent of all private and selfish interest."

Leaders Must Set an Example

Political leaders have to set a good example. No favoritism in the prosecution of wrongdoing should be tolerated and no double standards prevail. Exemplary public conduct is necessary for the respect and confidence people place in government. Unless it occurs at the top, one cannot expect to have good standards at lower levels.

Gerald Caiden, *USA Today*, July 1990.

Clearly, they were right. No matter how carefully we draft the laws, no matter how precisely we structure our democratic institutions, and no matter how meticulously we set up checks and balances, if we do not have leaders with high ethical standards the results can still be disastrous.

Applying a Higher Standard

I have come to the view that we *should* apply a higher standard of accountability to those seeking and holding public office than to those in private life. Are we thus applying a different standard of morality to public officials? In one sense, no. The kinds of standards we apply to public officials—such as veracity or fidelity—obviously apply to other people as well. However, because top government officials have both visibility and influence, my feeling is that we probably do, and should, apply a higher degree of accountability to their conduct. I think we are right to expect our leaders to reflect high personal integrity and exercise good judgment in both their public and private lives.

Although we need to make sure that we have people of high moral standards in office, my sense is that our efforts have generally been too one-sided. We focus our efforts on trying to "push out" of the process those whose standards of conduct do not quite measure up. This is, unfortunately, necessary at times. But to improve the standards in government, we must also try to "pull in" to the process Americans of fine character and sound judgment in both public and private matters.

We have an enormous pool of talented individuals with high

50

standards in this country. No doubt many of them are turned off to a career in public service. They are, rightly, concerned about: pleading with special interest groups to get the enormous sums of money needed to run for office; enduring harsh, negative campaigning and personal attacks; hearing their job portrayed as "dirty" and downgraded even by other politicians; deserting their families for the long months of running for elected office; answering questions from the media which poke and pry into every aspect of their personal lives; and having their real contributions ignored, while their minor mistakes are magnified.

These factors work against drawing good people into government service. We must work to reduce them and show that public service can be honorable.

Changing the major disincentives to public service in the American political system will certainly not be easy. But we must strive to make a career in politics and government service appealing and honorable.

We should tend to the wisdom of our Founding Fathers by consciously seeking to draw into politics people of virtue. If we do not succeed in doing this, we place in jeopardy our future. Government, like many other institutions, is only as good as the people who comprise it.

*"Our living former presidents could provide a
core of a new national council of experience."*

Seeking the Advice of Former Leaders Would Improve Leadership

Daniel J. Boorstin

In the following viewpoint, Daniel J. Boorstin argues that America can improve the quality of its leadership by creating a national council consisting of America's past presidents and other former leaders. Members of the council could bring their experience to bear on important matters of public policy, Boorstin continues. The policy solutions offered by the council would differ from those emanating from Congress and the White House because council members, having retired from politics, would be more concerned about the nation as a whole than with narrow political interests, Boorstin concludes. Boorstin, one of America's leading historians, is librarian emeritus of the Library of Congress.

As you read, consider the following questions:

1. How does America treat its older citizens, according to the author?
2. What does the British House of Lords contribute to public debate in Britain, according to Boorstin?
3. Do you share the author's optimism that the council would improve public debate and consideration of the nation's long-term problems? Why or why not?

Daniel J. Boorstin, "Saving a National Resource," a speech delivered to the conference Farewell to the Chief: The Role of Former Presidents in American Public Life at the Herbert Hoover Presidential Library, West Branch, Iowa, October 18, 1989.

Our American strength, we have often been told, has been our youth. Ours is, or until recently was, a young nation. "The youth of America," Oscar Wilde observed nearly a century ago, "is their oldest tradition. It has been going on now for three hundred years." It was the young in spirit, we say, who had the strength and will and the flexibility to leave an Old World to risk an Atlantic or Pacific passage for the uncertain promises of a still-uncharted America. The framers of the Constitution provided that a person thirty-five years of age was old enough to be president, a senator needed to be only thirty, a member of the House of Representatives only twenty-five, and the Twenty-Sixth Amendment to the Constitution lowered the voting age to 18. We have been ingenious, too, in devising institutions, like our Land Grant Colleges and the G.I. bill, to make the best use of our youth-resource.

But as our nation has matured, some would say only aged, as the need for immigrant courage is less general, and as life expectancy has increased, our population has been aging. And we have not shown the same enthusiasm and delight for old age. Our ingenuity in meeting the needs and opportunities and demands of youth has not been matched by any similar ingenuity in devising institutions to employ our older population. The late Senator Claude Pepper did a great service by focusing concern on the needs of the elderly. Though we have provided Golden Eagle passes for senior citizens to the national parks, we have run into gross political problems trying to provide health insurance especially for our aging citizens. The most conspicuous American institution directed to senior citizens is the so-called leisure city, a place not of creation but of recreation and vegetation. Our concern for the special needs of our ailing, idle, and disoriented aging has been admirable. But we need to refocus our attention on how to employ the special talents and resources of our most experienced citizens. . . .

Our Living Former Presidents

We now have four living former presidents, all happily functioning and in good health. This, I think, is a near record. In 1861 living former Presidents Van Buren, Tyler, Fillmore, Pierce, and Buchanan came to five. The number of living former presidents is likely to increase, with the decline of smoking and the increasing longevity of the American population, and especially since the Twenty-Second Amendment to the Constitution, which prevents a president from serving more than two terms.

The television spotlight on the sitting president has somehow deepened the penumbra into which a former president falls when he is no longer in the White House. Television has given a new meaning to the old proverb, "Out of sight, out of mind." Our failure to create a role in public life for former presidents is partly a reflection of our American preoccupation with youth, another symptom of our chronic ineptness in providing productive roles for older citizens. . . .

Jack Ohman. Reprinted by permission: Tribune Media Services.

One of the most distinctive and uncelebrated features of our American presidency has helped create the problem of the castaway president. The fixed four-year term makes a president's tenure different from that of a prime minister in a parliamentary system who can be turned out of office on short notice by a parliamentary majority or similarly brought back for a short period. Our fixed term has allowed our presidents to stay in office even when they have outlived their popularity with the electorate and even though they have no majority in either house of Congress, and so has given a prudent stability to the office. Especially since the Twenty-Second Amendment makes every president a lame duck in his second term, the constitutionally fixed term seems also to have defined a terminus to a president's active role in public life. A president, like other former holders of high office, is in danger of becoming what in Washington is called "a former person."

While almost everyone agrees that we are not making full use of the knowledge, wisdom, and experience of former presidents, there have been few practical suggestions of what should be done. The one repeatedly suggested (for example, by President Truman) that former presidents be given a non-voting role in the House of Representatives and/or Senate, has not invited wide approval or a serious initiative by the Congress. I do not join in the complaints of the ample financial and security provisions for former presidents. But the generous provision that Congress and the American people have made suggests a widespread belief that former presidents should not cease to play a role in our public life. . . . Perhaps at the time that we offer a new role for our former presidents we can find a way to bring more prominently into the public forum Americans of wisdom and experience in all fields.

The House of Lords

Our American need was dramatized for me when I was living in England and following parliamentary debates as reported in the London *Times*. I was not the only one to notice the superiority of the debates in the House of Lords over those in the House of Commons. The House of Lords, the unelected but elite second chamber of the British legislature, has little legislative power, despite its antiquity and prestige. But it has changed its character in recent years. Its hereditary membership has been overshadowed by the persons (many of them non-political) appointed for their recognized distinction and leadership in all areas of British life. The House [of Lords] has come to include economists like Barbara Ward, historians like Hugh Thomas and Asa Briggs, scientists like chemist Frederick Dainton. These people have earned their right to public respect and their right to be heard on public issues by their signal achievement in their own special field. Yet in the past they have had only the forum of their professional speciality, except for random interviews in the press, radio, and television incited less by public need than by desire of the media to fill space or time. Now that the character of the British second chamber has been changing, these people have a forum, where they can join in publicized debate on major public issues and where they can raise issues that they think have been neglected.

An additional qualification for membership in this group is that membership is a kind of certificate of withdrawal from the pursuit of elective office, which has made it an appropriate place, too, for former prime ministers, who are among the body's most valuable members.

It occurred to me to ask myself, and then to ask others, whether somehow we could devise an American institution, within our democratic tradition and our constitutional frame, to give us the benefits of a similar national forum. Obviously, heredity and aristocracy have no place in our country. But we too can benefit from a wider forum on national issues for our most experienced leaders in labor, business, science, literature, education, and the arts, for our citizens who have never been politicians, or have ceased to be politicians. Without authorization from anybody I have discussed this possibility in the last few years with a number of our leading citizens. I have found nearly unanimous agreement that there is something missing from our public life in this age of television.

An Abundance of Experience

Longer lives do not mean just more time spent in old age, but more time *before* old age as well. Americans have for many years been so focused on the joys of youth that we have often set too little value on experience. Now that so many of us will have so much more of it, we may come to see that wisdom is a precious commodity in itself.

D. Lydia Bronte, *The World & I*, December 1988.

What I offer is perhaps nothing more than the skeleton of an idea to stir our thinking toward creating a new national institution. National network television, with the auxiliaries in the cables, and the facilities of VHS, has provided unprecedented facilities for bringing together on the screen and in living rooms speakers who remain in widely separated places, and for allowing their words and ideas to reach unprecedented numbers. Now our nation can witness the exchanges of opinion and share the wisdom and experience of our best qualified leaders, not merely on political issues. Present uses of television as a forum are either for formal occasions, like the inauguration of a president or a campaign debate, with countless casual television interviews and encounters. May not the time have come to use this unprecedented technology for an unprecedented forum of leading experienced Americans? May not the time have come to give some rhythm . . . to such a forum, where citizens can follow the points of view of different leading Americans continuously and through time? . . .

A National Council of Experience

Our living former presidents could provide a core of a new national council of experience. A "House of Experience" and at this time they could solve an initial question—who will name the first members of the council? Perhaps each living former president could be asked to name three persons to join the group, which would bring the number to sixteen, for the present. As for other self-defining categories, former chief justices of the Supreme Court could be added. Perhaps, too, former speakers of the House of Representatives. Later, the group as a whole could be responsible for filling vacancies or adding members.

How often, where, and how should this national council of experience meet? There are many possibilities, and the proper rhythm and frequency of meetings will appear only when the group has begun to meet. To accomplish the purpose, to provide a continuing forum and continuing public interest, the meetings should be regular and not too infrequent. Perhaps the group could gather at least once a year in either Washington or at one of the presidential libraries. Other meetings could bring together some of the members as a kind of committee in their persons, and the whole group could quarterly exchange ideas and discuss through a televised forum from their separate places.

Who should set the agenda? Who could be better qualified to help us focus on enduring national issues than our former presidents with their experience and their feeling for the nation's unfinished business?

What sorts of topics should be on the agenda? The members would decide, but it would seem that the spotlight should be on long-term problems such as education, the relation of the United States to other countries and the world, the role and status of the family in American life, and the environment, rather than current questions of policy. The success of this national council would be tested by its ability to focus the experience and wisdom of leaders who are not seeking votes on matters of long-term national concern. And their ability to awaken interest in questions not in the headlines.

Unprecedented Opportunities

How could such a group be created? There are many possibilities. One would be an act of Congress chartering the council as a non-profit institution similar to the act chartering the American Historical Association. The national council should have no legal authority and no legislative role. It would be chartered to meet, discuss, and explore in public view the nation's long-term concerns. . . .

I am persuaded that we have the unprecedented opportunity created by our technology, and an unprecedented core resource in our former presidents. . . . With their wisdom and experience, and with the help of others we may be able to begin to fill a need in our public life.

Understanding Words
in Context

Readers occasionally come across words they do not recognize. And frequently, because they do not know a word or words, they will not fully understand the passage being read. Obviously, the reader can look up an unfamiliar word in a dictionary. By carefully examining the word in the context in which it is used, however, the word's meaning can often be determined. A careful reader may find clues to the meaning of the word in surrounding words, ideas, and attitudes.

Below are excerpts from the viewpoints in this chapter. In each excerpt, one of the words is printed in italized capital letters. Try to determine the meaning of each word by reading the excerpt. Under each excerpt you will find four definitions for the italicized word. Choose the one that is closest to your understanding of the word.

Finally, use a dictionary to see how well you have understood the words in context. It will be helpful to discuss with others the clues that helped you decide on each word's meaning.

1. Democratic government, if not controlled by constitutional or legislative *CONSTRAINTS*, has a tendency to grow into an unmanageable bureaucracy.

   CONSTRAINTS means:

   a) guardians   c) restrictions
   b) excesses   d) debates

2. *MANDATED* rotation in office through term limitation will make elections more competitive and interesting.

   MANDATED means:

   a) unethical   c) markedly uneven
   b) legally ordered   d) unauthorized

3. This is the *PARADOX*: Despite a deep dissatisfaction with Congress, the American people are reelecting their congressional representatives at the highest rate in history.

   PARADOX means:

   a) contradiction   c) victory
   b) good news   d) difficulty

4. The Constitutional Convention considered limiting legislators' eligibility for reelection but the Convention *EXPUNGED* the limitation less than a month after it was proposed.

   EXPUNGED means:

   a) changed   c) established
   b) erased   d) extended

5. To find a friendly face amid the "faceless" bureaucrats and a helping hand in the midst of injustice, citizens began to turn to their legislator for *SUCCOR*.

   SUCCOR means:

   a) entertainment   c) money
   b) candy   d) aid

6. No matter how cautiously we draft the laws, no matter how precisely we structure our democratic institutions, and no matter how *METICULOUSLY* we set up checks and balances, if we do not have leaders with high ethical standards the results can still be disastrous.

   METICULOUSLY means:

   a) blamelessly   c) loosely
   b) stupidly   d) carefully

7. Our failure to create a role in public life for former presidents is partly a reflection of our American preoccupation with youth, another symptom of our chronic *INEPTNESS* in providing productive roles for older citizens.

   INEPTNESS means:

   a) competency   c) condition
   b) laziness   d) carefulness

8. Washington is a city where a permanent *ELITE* holds sway, where politicians and their accomplices control the money and prestige that political power can bring.

   ELITE means:

   a) party atmosphere   c) privileged group
   b) narrow view   d) minority group

Periodical Bibliography

The following articles have been selected to supplement the diverse views presented in this chapter.

Eleanor Clift	"Term Limits Won't Work," *Newsweek,* November 11, 1991.
Tristram Coffin	"Misconduct in Washington," *The Washington Spectator,* October 1, 1991. Available from PO Box 20065, London Terrace Station, New York, NY 10011.
Ethics: Easier Said than Done	Entire issue on political ethics, Issue 13, 1991. Available from 310 Washington Blvd., Suite 104, Marina del Rey, CA 90292.
Samuel Francis	"No Easy Path for Movement to Limit Terms," *Insight,* December 2, 1991. Available from PO Box 91022, Washington, DC 20090-1022.
John H. Fund	"Term Limitation: An Idea Whose Time Has Come," *Policy Analysis,* October 30, 1990. Available from the Cato Institute, 224 Second St. SE, Washington, DC 20003.
Gary M. Galles	"Term-of-Office Limits Won't Reduce Government Abuse," *The Freeman,* March 1991. Available from the Foundation for Economic Education, Inc., Irvington-on-Hudson, NY 10533.
Meg Greenfield	"Everyone vs. Congress," *Newsweek,* November 11, 1991.
Brooks Jackson	"Electoral Detox: A Twelve-Step Cure for Donor Dependency," *The American Prospect,* Fall 1991. Available from New Prospect, Inc., PO Box 7645, Princeton, NJ 08543.
Michael Kinsley	"It's Your Fault," *The New Republic,* October 28, 1991.
Roger Koopman	"Morality and Our Public Servants," *The New American,* September 24, 1991. Available from 770 Westhill Blvd., Appleton, WI 54915.
James L. Payne	"Bad Influence," *Reason,* August/September 1991.
Mark P. Petracca	"The Poison of Professional Politics," *Policy Analysis,* May 10, 1991.
Nelson W. Polsby	"Constitutional Mischief: What's Wrong with Term Limitations," *The American Prospect,* Summer 1991.
George F. Will	"A Case for Term Limits," *Newsweek,* October 21, 1991.

How Can Voter Participation Be Increased?

Chapter Preface

For years, political analysts used voting percentages as a primary indicator of Americans' interest in politics and government. Consequently, when it became evident that Americans were avoiding the polls in great numbers—for example, an estimated two-thirds of those eligible did not vote in the 1990 congressional elections—many people voiced their concerns that Americans had grown apathetic. These concerns led political analysts to examine the reasons for the decline in voting and to debate the importance of voting in the American political process.

Those most concerned about voting's decline believe the trend undermines democracy. Analysts say that if citizens neglect to vote, they rob themselves of their power and ability to influence government decisions and leaders. In effect, they give up their right to democracy, and they allow the nation to be ruled by a small group of people in Washington, D.C. As noted activist Jesse Jackson states, "Meaningful democracy in the United States is languishing because of . . . declining popular participation." Jackson and others point out that the United States has the lowest rate of voter participation of any democracy in the world. "How can we hold ourselves out to the rest of the world as the fountain of democracy," Jackson asks, "when we have a lower rate of voter participation than Panama, Nicaragua, the Soviet Union and every Western European democracy?" Jackson believes that if American democracy is to be saved Americans must return to the polls.

But not all political analysts are as concerned as Jackson. Voter turnout is not "a measure of the health of the republic," University of California at Berkeley political scientist Raymond E. Wolfinger argues. He cites the fact that Switzerland has a lower voter turnout rate than the United States and yet "is one of the best governed countries in the world." Wolfinger and his supporters believe that many factors, including Americans' high participation in special interest groups, must be considered in any evaluation of the state of American democracy. "To say that voting is the only barometer of civic virtue is to betray a very narrow perspective. . . . Participation in public life can be defined more broadly," columnist Mona Charen asserts. Wolfinger, Charen, and others downplay the importance of voting and maintain that decreased voter turnout may actually be an indication of Americans' contentment. Americans may not vote because they do not want change.

Whether the decline in voting is a sign of contentment or of apathy and dissatisfaction is just one of several issues debated in the following chapter.

*"A major explanation for low turnout in the
United States is the comparative difficulty of
registration here."*

Ease Voter Registration
Requirements

Raymond E. Wolfinger

In contrast to Britain, the United States places the responsibility
for registering to vote on the individual citizen. Many critics
blame this for the reason why many Americans do not vote. In
the following viewpoint, Raymond E. Wolfinger argues that sim-
plifying the registration process will increase the number of registered voters and thereby increase voter turnout. Wolfinger is a
professor of political science at the University of California at
Berkeley and the co-author of *Who Votes?*

As you read, consider the following questions:

1. How does Wolfinger refute arguments that Americans are
   apathetic and uninterested in politics?
2. How does Britain simplify voting registration, according to
   the author?
3. In Wolfinger's opinion, why are Republicans opposed to
   measures easing registration requirements?

Raymond E. Wolfinger, "Voter Turnout," *Society*, July/August 1991. Reprinted with
permission.

Individual beliefs about government, politics, and politicians often are not related to variations in electoral participation. This generalization holds true in two respects. First, in international comparisons. Low voter turnout in the United States is not explained by the comparative level of Americans' interest in politics, their degree of trust in the government, or any other attitude toward political institutions and actors. Second, the largest group of light voters in the United States, amounting to nearly a third of all citizens, is just as politically motivated as the rest of the population, whose turnout is much greater.

Low turnout is always a moderately big story during election campaigns, but unfortunately people who discuss it usually draw the wrong conclusions: Americans are such light voters because they are bored by politics, alienated, mistrustful of politicians, and/or suspicious of the political system. Presumably, so the story goes, Europeans are not like this; this is why we find 94 percent turnout in Italy, 89 percent in Austria and Belgium, and so on.

Myth Versus Fact

The facts are different. Thirty years ago, Gabriel Almond and Sidney Verba reported, in *The Civic Culture*, the first comparative study of attitudes toward the political process in several countries. One of the questions they asked respondents was what aspects of their countries made them proud. Eighty-five percent of Americans said they were proud of our political system, the Constitution, and similar political subjects. In Italy, where nearly everyone votes, just 3 percent of the sample took pride in any aspect of their political system.

More recent research has explored relevant comparative attitudes in several ways. As far as satisfaction with their political system is concerned, the most contented people are the Swiss. Americans are a bit less satisfied; at the other end of the continuum are the Italians. When it comes to interest in politics, Americans consistently rank highest. Asked how pessimistic they would be about having an effect on politics if they were themselves to become involved, Americans and Germans were the least pessimistic, Austrians were the most. Asked about their own political efficacy, Americans and Greeks scored highest, Belgians the lowest. In short, if motivations predicted the level of turnout in each country, the United States, rather than being next to last, would lead the pack.

Americans usually measure turnout as the proportion of the voting-age population—citizens and non-citizens alike—who go to the polls. By this yardstick our voting rate is indeed low. (As the non-citizen proportion of the population grows, this method progressively will underestimate turnout because the denominator

64

of the percentage computation will include more and more people who cannot vote.)

How would American turnout look if the yardstick used was the one normally used in Europe: the turnout of the registered? This figure could be estimated for each American state by dividing the total number of votes cast by the number of people on the state's registration records. But this method would seriously underestimate the true figure because of the "deadwood" on registration rolls: names of people who have moved. Most states try to clean their records by removing people who have not voted for several years, but the mobility rate in the United States is so high that this effort inevitably runs several years behind, hence the deadwood.

Bill Day. Reprinted by permission: Tribune Media Services.

A more valid measure of the turnout of the registered is provided by the University of Michigan National Election Studies,whose interviewers verify each respondent's claims about registration and voting by inspecting county records. This method reveals that 84 to 87 percent of registered Americans went to the polls in the three presidential elections of the 1980s. By this measure, the United States does not look nearly as bad in world turnout comparisons—eleventh place, just eight percentage points below the leading nation and thirty-eight points better than the worst one.

This suggests, of course, that a major explanation for low turnout in the United States is the comparative difficulty of registration here. In a few democratic countries, voting is compulsory; that is, nonvoters are subject to a fine. The fine is not very large, however, and the list of acceptable excuses is lengthy. The effect of the legal obligation seems to be moral rather than an actual financial incentive.

By far the most widespread system is automatic registration. In most European countries, the law requires that citizens tell the local authorities where they live. When people move from one place to another, they are required by law to report their new address. The civic register maintained by these requirements is also an electoral register. If one is a law-abiding citizen, one is automatically registered to vote.

Voting is not compulsory in Italy, but registration is automatic and the constitution states that it is the duty of every citizen of the Republic to vote. Nonvoters are liable to having their papers stamped with the notation that they did not vote. Moreover, the Italian government provides subsidized train tickets to people wishing to return to their villages in order to vote. As one might imagine, this means that elections are for many Italians an occasion for going home and visiting their families.

There is no automatic registration in the United Kingdom, but the government conducts an annual electoral canvass. Every household is sent a form and instructions to list all adult members of the household for the purpose of compiling an electoral register. Non-responding households are visited by canvassers. In Canada, provincial governments subsidize the two leading political parties in each constituency to conduct a door-to-door canvass before each election to compile an electoral register. The American system imposes the responsibility for registration on the individual citizen. In some places it is easier to register; in other places, harder. Doubtless everybody knows somebody interested in politics who could not easily find out how to register and was therefore unable to vote.

Registered Voters' Turnout Is High

In America, not only is turnout very high among the registered in the aggregate, but it is high among groups of registered citizens who are usually considered light voters. For example, Americans who have never seen the inside of a high school classroom have a 51 percent turnout rate, compared to 84 percent for people with at least one year of postgraduate education; the gap between the two groups is 33 percentage points. But among Americans who are registered to vote, people with no high school education have a 79 percent turnout rate, compared to 96 percent for those with postgraduate work; a gap of 17 percentage points.

It is well known that young people are light voters and that turnout gradually increases as people get older. Among the registered, however, there is no difference between age groups in the proportion of those who vote. People under the age of twenty-five will, if they are registered, vote at the same rate as those who are fifty-five. By the same token, people who profess to have no interest at all in politics will, if they are registered, vote at a 74 percent rate. Pondering the likelihood that people who are registered are very likely indeed to vote in presidential elections, one might well consider what life experiences militate against being registered.

By far the most important of these experiences is moving. The last Census Bureau study of residential mobility revealed that fully 20 percent of all Americans had not lived at the same address for as long as one year. In 1980, one-third of all adults had not lived at the same address for two years. (This discussion will center on the 1980 elections since one of the best sources of data on voter turnout, the *Voter Supplement of the Current Population Survey*, unfortunately did not ask about residential mobility between 1980 and 1990.) In 1980, 48 percent of people who had not lived in the same place for two years reported that they voted, compared to 65 percent of those who had stayed put for longer. Sophisticated multivariate analysis of these data reveal that this is not merely a statistical artifact. People who recently changed residence are less likely to vote largely for that reason: the length of time they have lived at their current address.

This brings us to the second limit on motivation as an explanation of turnout: The movers, those who have not lived at their present address for two years, are no less interested, informed, attentive, or involved in politics than the other two-thirds of the population; but they are considerably less likely to vote. They are lighter voters because they have not gotten around to registering. If we look at residential mobility over a broader time span, we find that the longer people have lived at their current address, the more likely they are to vote. The reason is clear. When people move, many tasks are more important than registering to vote. Half of all moves take place during the summer. If people move in the summer of an election year, they only have about a month before the deadline for registration, which in most places is thirty days before the election. If they move in a non-election year, there is no great stimulus to register.

Increasing Voter Turnout

If one were interested in increasing voter turnout in the United States, the implications for action are fairly obvious. For one thing, there is not much point in fooling around with nostrums like making election day a holiday, holding elections on Sunday, keeping the polls open for twenty-four hours, and so on. Such steps could affect only the small minority of the registered who do not vote now. Those who believe that the way to increase turnout is to get more people registered are on the right track.

Difficult Registration Lowers Turnout

In the last 30 years, voting participation has declined almost 12 percent. In the last presidential election, only slightly more than half the eligible voters actually went to the polls. Many factors are responsible for the drop-off in voting, some of which are beyond our control. Higher voter turnout levels can't be legislatively mandated.

But we can do something about by far the most important factor, which is registration. The simple fact of the matter is, you cannot vote if you are not registered, and for many Americans today, getting registered just is not very easy. Indeed, when people who didn't vote in 1988 were asked why, the reason given most often was not being registered.

Al Swift, *Congressional Digest*, April 1990.

Most promising among light voters are the movers, since their failure to vote is not so much due to weak motivation as to administrative considerations. (Of course, people who are passionately interested in politics will probably put registering to vote near the top of their agenda when they move, but the vast majority of people are not passionate about politics.) The most useful approach here is to consider what kinds of things people who move are likely to do, and then link the registration process to those routine actions. People who move usually have to worry about getting a telephone and arranging for electric power, gas, and water. These interactions provide opportunities for the providers of those services to assist the new residents with registration-by-mail forms.

The most promising approach is to exploit connections that movers have with government agencies. One example is filing change-of-address notices with the post office, which almost everyone does in order to continue receiving mail. About 40 million such notices are filed each year. This form could be modified to obtain slightly more information and to produce a second copy automatically. For intrastate movers who were already registered (83 percent of all moves are inside the same state), the second copy would be turned over to local voting officials, who would transfer the registration from the old to the new address. This is not a way to register people anew, but to maintain the status of those who are already registered. It would also remove deadwood by cancelling the old-address registration, a feature that appeals to election of officials.

In 1985 and 1987 bills to require the Postal Service to use such a modified change-of-address notice in any state that wished to make proper use of it were introduced in Congress by Representative Mel Levine (D-Cal.). Eventually the Levine Bill was co-sponsored by ninety representatives, mostly, but not exclusively, Democrats. It was endorsed by the National Association of Counties and other interest groups, supported by members of the Democratic House leadership, and twice reported by the subcommittee that considered it. And twice it died in the full Committee on Post Office and Civil Service, a victim of the Postal Service's intense hostility and, perhaps, of a cool attitude by voting rights groups.

Other Measures

A more comprehensive measure, based in part on the previously described findings, came close to succeeding in the 101st Congress. The National Voter Registration Act, designed by Representatives Al Swift (D-Wash.) and Bill Thomas (R-Cal.), the chairman and ranking minority member of the Subcommittee on Elections of the Committee on House Administration, provided, among other things, that reports of address changes to state departments of motor vehicles be used to update voter registration. Moreover, the bill gave states two options to keep their registration lists current. One alternative was using the Postal Service's computerized change-of-address data file, which is publicly available. States choosing this option would automatically re-register all people moving within the same county, a majority of all movers.

Unlike the Levine bill, this measure was considered in a friendly committee environment. By the time it reached the House floor in February 1990 it had 120 cosponsors, including the Speaker, two committee chairmen, and three of the five top members of the Republican leadership. At the last minute it was opposed by the White House and the House minority leader, Robert Michel (R-Ill.), which came as something of a shock after the year-long bipartisan harmony in which the bill had been drafted. The bill easily passed the House later that month, supported by almost all Democrats and a third of all Republicans.

The Senate bill, although nearly identical to the House version, had no Republican cosponsors. When the leadership finally brought it to the floor in late September 1990, it fell five votes short of the 60 needed to overcome Republican filibuster. Only two Republican senators voted to impose closure and two Democrats voted not to. In April 1991, the Senate Committee on

Rules and Administration supported, by a 7-4 vote, what was essentially the same bill that had failed the previous September. This time, however, it had a Republican cosponsor and therefore, perhaps, a better chance than its predecessor.

Why Do Republicans Oppose Reform?

The data that yielded the findings about the relationship of mobility to turnout can be analyzed to provide several answers to that question. If the effect of mobility on turnout were totally eliminated, voter participation in presidential elections would rise 9 percentage points. Although a substantial increase, this would still leave the United States in next to last place in international comparisons. This higher turnout would not produce an advantage of consequence for either party. The hypothetically larger electorate would be 2 percent more Independent, at the expense of Republicans. Most Independents vote for the winning presidential candidate, so the net Republican loss would be less than one percent. Elections have been decided by narrower margins, but this difference is much smaller than the margin of error in any survey.

Republicans oppose reform measures like the Swift-Thomas bill that appear to be politically neutral because they are unconvinced by research evidence and still hold to the old belief that higher turnout favors Democratic candidates. Republicans are also more concerned about economy in government and election fraud. Fraud is a real problem only where an organization can exploit opportunities wholesale and most such organizations are Democratic. Therefore Republicans are skeptical of proposals that would impose higher administrative costs on local officials and expand opportunities for fraudulent registrations. The drawback to this notion is that proposals to re-register movers inevitably would cancel their old-address registration. The resulting clean and current registration lists reduce election costs and opportunities for fraudulent use of deadwood.

A third explanation may be closer to the mark. At least one of the approaches to re-registering movers in the Swift-Thomas bill can be used for its own selective purposes by a single political party. The Postal Service's National Change of Address data are available for purchase from authorized vendors. In California these data can be merged with computerized voter registration data, which include the registrant's political affiliation, to produce a data set with the names and addresses of all the newly-arrived Republicans (or Democrats) in any or all parts of the state. In states where registration is not by party, ZIP code classification provides a rough surrogate measure. To the extent that Republicans can do for themselves what measures like the Swift-Thomas bill would do for everyone, they may be motivated to oppose such reforms.

"Declining voter turnout [has] occurred precisely during the time that television has become a central factor . . . in the conduct of the nation's politics."

Regulate TV Campaign Ads

Curtis B. Gans

Most Americans receive information on political candidates by watching televised campaign ads. In the following viewpoint, Curtis B. Gans contends that these ads contribute to the decrease in voter participation. Negative, superficial, and inaccurate campaign ads, Gans believes, cause Americans to lose faith in their political leaders and in the value of voting. If the government regulated these ads, it could improve Americans' opinion of politicians and thereby increase political participation. Gans is the director of the Committee for the Study of the American Electorate, a research organization that studies Americans' political participation.

As you read, consider the following questions:

1. What evidence does Gans give to show that negative campaign advertising harms voter turnout?
2. How has the increase in television advertising affected the cost of political campaigns, according to the author?

Curtis B. Gans, testimony before the U.S. Senate Committee on Commerce, Science, and Transportation, Subcommittee on Communications, July 19, 1989.

In 1988, we held a Presidential election and nearly half the eligible electorate stayed home. The United States had the lowest turnout since 1924 and, outside of the states of the old Confederacy we had the lowest turnout since 1824. Turnout declined among every age, income, racial, ethnic, level of educational attainment and occupational group with the exception of those aged 65-70.

Since the 1960's, turnout in both Presidential and mid-term elections has declined by more than 20 percent nationally and by more than 30 percent outside of the South. More than 20 million Americans who were formerly voters, no longer bother to cast their ballots. Young citizens, aged 18-24, voted at a 29 percent rate in 1988, at a 16.6 percent rate in 1986.

The United States, if one counts both its Presidential elections and its mid-term elections, now has the lowest rate of voter participation of any democracy in the world.

Since 1974, campaign spending for the U.S. House of Representatives has jumped from $53.5 million to $256.5 million. Spending in races for the U.S. Senate has increased from $34.7 million in 1974 to $201.2 million in 1988. These figures represent a nearly 600 percent increase in campaign costs in a decade and a half or, in constant dollars, more than a 300 percent increase.

Both of these phenomena—spiralling campaign costs and declining voter turnout—have occurred precisely during the time that television has become a central factor in American lives and in the conduct of the nation's politics. It is my considered judgment, based on 14 years of study in this field, that this juxtaposition—the rise of television, the increase in campaign costs and the decline in citizen civic involvement—is not coincidental.

No Regulations of TV Campaigns

The United States is also the only democracy in the world which does not, either by time or format, regulate its televised political advertising. The United States also has substantially lower turnout than any other democracy. And it is my considered judgment that the juxtaposition of these factors—the lack of regulation of television advertising in the United States and its substantially lower turnout—is not coincidental.

Reasonable people may disagree as to which form of constructive regulation of political advertising on television will be most effective, offers the best chance of enactment and can pass Constitutional muster. . . .

But the critical question now is not the form of such legislative regulation but whether there will be such regulation at all. For until and unless there is such legislation and regulation, it is likely that the conduct of politics in what prides itself as the best and greatest democracy in the world will continue to set an example, except in time of war, recession or in the presence of an overwhelmingly charismatic candidate, for the greatest percentage of voters driven from the polls and for a government of, for and by the intensely interested few.

It is within this framework that one may view examples of the current state of American politics.

Problems Caused by Negative Campaign Ads

With regard to these ads there are five things to be noted:

• Negative, trivial and scurrilous ads are not a new phenomenon nor are present versions necessarily more outrageous than those from other elections. What is different is not the type but the volume. Where such ads were once limited to the occasional campaign and accompanied by howls of outrage or put on largely by independent expenditure groups, they are now the staple of all campaigns for which television can be used as a primary medium of communications.

• These ads . . . that disgrace the airwaves each election are at best oversimplified and misleading, at worst and often, distorted and downright dishonest. Because of this they present a necessarily false picture of the issues, the character of the candidate and, to a captive public—since these ads are designed to be shown in the midst of programming the public is interested [in]—a negative image of the political enterprise as a whole.

• They have become the staple of campaigns because the independent, non-responsible and increasingly irresponsible political consultants who today run American campaigns say they work to win elections. But if the truth be told, they work for only 50 percent of the consultants and candidates who win while 100 percent of the electorate which has to view these ads becomes the loser.

• These ads emerge from the same technological development, the tracking poll. When the consultant for candidate A finds through the tracking poll that the candidate for whom he or she works is substantially behind candidate B, he orders up a set of demagogic attack ads to cast doubts about the opponent, loosen candidate B's hold on the electorate and reduce the impulse to vote for B. What happens, as a consequence, is that the consultant for candidate B notes through his tracking polls that the gap between the two candidates is closing, has closed or that A has overtaken B. And in order to restore B's primacy, he orders up a dose of the same medicine. He does so because the nature of the ads used against B are virtually unanswerable, appealing, as they are intended to do, to the emotions rather than reason. The only recourse is to respond in kind. The result is an escalating arms race of attack ads that becomes the equivalent of airwave pollution. And the impression that the electorate gets is that all politicians and the political process as a whole are not worthy of their respect and trust.

• These ads, in turn determine the nature of the entire campaign, for they establish the themes around which the campaign is conducted. If we have campaigns that are increasingly 30- and 60-second spot advertising, seven-second sound-bites and candidates who seem unable to say an unprogrammed word, it stems from a single source—campaigns that are run almost exclusively on television by irresponsible political consultants who, in the pursuit of winning, know of no tactic too low or trivial to besmirch their opposition and drive down the opponent's turnout. Does anyone seriously believe that the 1988 Presidential election was or should have been about Pledges of Allegiance, "good jobs for good wages, prison furlough programs, or competence?". . .

Ed Gamble. Reprinted with permission.

For the overwhelming majority of campaigns, what the public sees is a set of virtually indistinguishable (in type) ads which cast aspersions on all candidates and invite the response the public is increasingly witnessing. The electorate is voting with their bottoms—they are turning off, tuning out and sitting out elections in ever-increasing numbers and frequency. . . .

All of which is to suggest strongly that this is a problem which must be addressed head-on. It must be addressed head-on because of a number of important and specific threats to the health and welfare of American democracy. . . .

Turnout Should Increase

While, in part due to my not so gentle ministrations in the field of publicity, it has become generally known that American turnout is low and has been declining for nearly three decades. . . .

One of the best academic books on the causes of declining voter turnout in America, Ruy Teixeira's *Why Americans Don't Vote*, traces three primary causes for the decline in participation: 1. a decline in citizen feelings of efficacy about their vote or whether their vote makes a difference; 2. a decline in allegiance to and strong feelings for either of the two major political parties; and 3. a decline in newspaper reading as a primary source of information about politics.

Could it be that, in part, underlying each of these causes lies the rise of political advertising on television—1. in the increasing demagoguery and trivialization of our politics that makes the perceived stakes not worth the effort to participate; 2. in parties without enduring messages or messages that are determined by pollsters and hucksters at any given moment; and 3. in information fed in short messages and sound bites which bear little relation to the concerns of the citizen or the problems they see?

Cost of Campaigns

There is no question that the spiralling cost of campaigns is directly attributable to the increased use of television advertising in general and the widespread belief that demagogic advertising works.

My committee has been tracking spending on the five most expensive campaigns for the U.S. Senate in each election year since 1974 and for the competitive Senate races since that year. Some sample returns from these studies might be instructive:

• In 1974, the average cost of the five most expensive Senatorial campaigns was $1 million or $0.67 a vote. By 1984, the average cost was $10 million or $7.74 a vote.

• In 1974, the average amount spent on television advertising in the campaigns was $350,000 or $0.12 a vote. In 1984, the average spent on political advertising on television was $5 million or $3.40 a vote.

• In these most expensive campaigns overall costs increased ten-fold (five-fold in constant dollars), while media spending increased more than 30-fold (more than 15-fold in constant dollars).

• The increase in media spending, it should be noted, was

more than double the increase in rates charged for political advertising. . . .

- In 1974, candidates in competitive races for the U.S. Senate spent nearly $8 million overall (a little less than $1 million per race) and approximately $0.66 a vote. They spent $0.21 a vote on media.
- In 1986, candidates in competitive races spent more than $50 million (or more than $8 million a race). This resulted in a cost of $4.18 per vote in overall spending and $2.27 per vote in media spending.
- In 1988, candidates in competitive Senate races spent nearly $53 million overall (more than $7 million a race). They spent $4.41 a vote overall and $2.55 a vote for media.

Thus, in competitive races overall cost has increased about seven-fold while costs attributable to media have increased nearly 13-fold (3.5-fold and 6.7-fold in constant dollars.)

The conclusion is inescapable. Unless the use of television in the modern campaign is brought under some reasonable control, access to politics will only be available to those who either possess great wealth or have access to and are potentially beholden to such wealth.

At a time when partisan perceptions of self-interest prohibit agreement on other aspects of campaign finance reform, regulation of television advertising, in view of its pernicious effects regardless of person or party, may be the only way to begin to end the upward spiral of campaign costs.

Allocation of Campaign Resources

One nexus between the impact of political advertising on campaign cost and the impact on turnout lies in the allocation of campaign resources.

In 1974 competitive Senate campaigns allocated 31 percent of their resources to political advertising. In 1988 more than 57.9 percent of every campaign dollar was allocated to television advertising. These figures are exclusive of fund raising costs.

This means that for the average campaign for which television is seen by the consultant who runs as the primary tool for its conduct, nearly 90 percent of the campaign budget is devoted to television advertising or fund raising for it.

This, in turn, leaves only 10 percent of the campaign budget for such things as candidate travel, speech writing, press and public relations and staff. And it means that nothing or next to nothing is spent on any activity that involves the citizenry.

It is thus no wonder that we have developed the political equivalent of the Silent Spring in American politics, in which there are no longer buttons and bumper stickers, phone banks and field organizations, volunteers and participants. We manipulate our citizens, we do not involve them.

If, as political scientist Ruy Teixeira has suggested, one of the principal reasons for declining turnout is decline in allegiance to the major political parties, then this too can in part, be traced to political advertising.

For, on the one hand it used to be true that candidates were nurtured by the party, trained by its leadership to state and national leadership, dependent on local party organization for electoral success and beholden to the party once in office in such a way that permitted some discipline on principle and program. Now, a candidate seeks money, a pollster and a media advisor and arrives in Washington, dependent only on polls and constituent service for his continuance in office.

The Effects of Negative Ads

Although many candidates rightly insist they discuss serious issues, they usually don't do so where it matters—on paid TV commercials. These are increasingly devoted to pushing hot-button issues, sugarcoating the candidate's résumé or trashing his opposition. Increasingly, candidates launch a preemptive strike to "drive up the negative" before rivals established a positive identification in voters' minds.

Richard Moe, *Los Angeles Times*, August 19, 1990.

On the other hand, once the parties stood for some core of policy and principle. Now their advocacy, nationally and locally, is determined by the same pollsters and media advisors that run individual campaigns. The parties have become little more than campaign service agencies and both individually and collectively there is little reason for enduring citizen allegiance to either candidate or party.

This transcendance of party in favor of media consultants enhances the centrifugal force of special interests, weakens the forces of popular mobilization, both within parties and among other organizations and lessens what little stability and cohesion exists within the American political system.

Effects on Policy

It can also be said that the current system of campaigning through consultants, polls and demagogic advertising weakens the impulse to political leadership.

When once it was the business of leadership to determine what policies were right and wise and then find ways of educating the electorate to their enactment and implementation, it is now the custom to poll the electorate to find out what to say in the first place. Policy, thus, is too often determined by poll rather than by principle or need.

This, in turn, has the effect of restricting policy options. Reasonable people can disagree about whether Social Security was intended as an inalienable right for all Americans and therefore should not be tampered with or whether it was intended as insurance for those less fortunate and thus can and should be either taxed or means tested. But in the face of the potential of a demagogic commercial showing a poor grandmotherly looking woman with a voice-over saying, Senator X voted to cut your mother's Social Security, the debate over Social Security's future never gets beyond a narrow range. . . .

The same principles apply with regard to the political marketplace. . . .

We, of course, do not know how many Americans capable of great leadership have chosen not to run because of something that they have once said or done might be taken out of context, used and magnified in a demagogic advertisement and served to ruin, unnecessarily, their personal, professional and political reputations. But we do know that the present system of distorted and demagogic advertisements cannot help but serve to restrict citizen choice and constrict the reservoir of political leadership. . . .

Conversely, increased dependence on demagogic televised advertising which enhances the power and influence of media consultants detracts from the ability to hold office-holders accountable.

A media consultant is not by nature accountable to the electorate. He or she makes his or her living and insures his future by winning elections for the clients he or she is hired by. He or she can and does use whatever techniques and stratagems are likely to benefit the candidate whether those strategies and tactics are ethical or not.

By using techniques such as actors playing parts, demagogic scene setting, impersonal voice-overs, anonymous commentators, emotional music, etc., the consultant can and increasingly frequently does establish the terms of debate in such a way that the client escapes responsibility for what is conveyed and in terms that are unanswerable by the opposition, except by resorting to precisely the same techniques.

So what has developed in these United States is a competition, not between parties, principles, proposals or candidates, but between media advisors who compete with each other to see who can outslick the other and win. And in the continued absence of candidates with the courage or character to tell these consultants that they are ruining our political system and that they ought to shut up and go home, the public has no one to hold accountable.

*"Real debate holds political rewards. Should
that occur, there will be a . . . more informed,
participating citizenry. "*

Improve Public Debate

Barry Sussman

Barry Sussman is a polling analyst and the author of *What
Americans Really Think*, from which this viewpoint is excerpted.
Sussman argues that America's politicians do not inform the
public about important issues and do not encourage public debate. Most politicians view the public with distrust and skepti-
cism, Sussman believes, and therefore are reluctant to engage
citizens in meaningful debate. Because of this, most citizens are
so poorly informed that they tend to withdraw from politics and
develop an unhealthy cynicism toward government. By improving the quality of public debate, leaders could develop a more
informed, participating citizenry with a greater interest in voting, Sussman concludes.

As you read, consider the following questions:

1. What were the findings of Sussman's experiment using a
   Washington Post/ABC News poll?
2. What was Thomas Jefferson's opinion of the tension between
   government and public opinion in a democracy, according to
   the author?

It is impossible for even extremely concerned citizens, let alone ordinary ones, to come to intelligent judgments on many public-policy issues. Their own experience is too circumscribed and the leaders they look to are unhelpful, unwilling to bring to the fore even excruciating national problems.

Thus the matter of unemployment . . . is important mostly to the jobless or the marginally employed, but not to average working people. Life-threatening toxic-waste dumps should be a major concern but are not much more than an abstraction to most Americans. Foreign-policy decisions that shape the world's future engage the average person only when it looks like someone in the family may be called to arms; for the most part they stay off to the side. In just such a manner was the Vietnam war fought for many years.

The need for people to be active in public affairs was seen as crucial by Thomas Jefferson, who wrote in a 1789 letter that "every government degenerates when trusted to the rulers of the people alone." The caution is still valid two hundred years later.

Surely, people should pay more attention to politics than they do, even without prodding by leaders. But it is understandable if they do not. Most have enough difficulty getting by from day to day in coping with their own problems; they cannot wade through the web of confusion spun by political leaders. They need some help and encouragement.

Jefferson came back to the theme in 1820, again in a letter, writing, "I know of no safe depository of the ultimate powers of the society but the people themselves; and if we think them not enlightened enough to exercise their control with a wholesome discretion, the remedy is not to take it from them, but to inform their discretion by education."

Testing the Theory

A little test I conducted in a *Washington Post/ABC News* poll in December, 1983, demonstrates how loose the ties are for most people when it comes to political convictions and ideas, and how strongly debate, even minimal debate, can sway many of them.

Typically in our polls we would ask the presidential-popularity question—"Do you approve or disapprove of the way Ronald Reagan is handling his job as president?"—right off the bat, as the first or second item.

The reasoning was that in such a way the people we interviewed would give their first impressions of Reagan, allowing us to track a genuine trend from month to month, year to year. Had we asked this question in the middle or toward the end of a poll, some people's responses might have been influenced by the line of thinking advanced by previous questions. We could have thrown in a few hardballs, asking, for example, about Reagan's support for James Watt in the early days of his presidency, or the Iran arms deal in the latter stages, creating a sort of brainwashing effect. It is easy for a pollster to bounce the results around intentionally by setting up respondents in this manner through what is called a "question-order bias," or "question-order effect."

© Liederman/Rothco. Reprinted with permission.

In December, 1983, with the agreement of our colleagues at *ABC News*, I altered our procedure. We asked the approval-rating question first, as usual, but then we asked it again, toward the end of the interview. In line with our standard format, we asked people not only whether they approved or disapproved, but whether they felt that way "strongly" or "somewhat."

We interviewed 1,506 people in the survey, and in response to our first question, twenty-nine percent said they approved Reagan's handling of the presidency strongly, thirty percent approved somewhat, fifteen percent disapproved somewhat, twenty-two percent disapproved strongly, and four percent expressed no opinion. The overall fifty-nine-percent approval rating was in the "good" range—not outstanding but safely above the danger point for a president.

The survey then asked opinions on a wide variety of issues: Reagan's handling of the economy, foreign affairs, relations with the Soviet Union, the situation in Lebanon, the federal budget deficit. These were followed by more questions on the economy, on Lebanon, on Democratic candidates for the presidency, on

81

preferences between the leading Democrats and Reagan, and on a number of other matters.

Finally, question number sixty-one went back to the presidential-popularity item, with this preface read by interviewers: "I've asked you some questions on how Reagan has handled a number of issues. With that in mind, let me repeat one of the first questions I asked. Do you approve or disapprove of the way Reagan is handling his job as president?" Again, people also were asked if they approved or disapproved "strongly" or "somewhat."

At a glance, the differences were so small as to appear nonexistent: fifty-nine percent approved, the same as in the first instance, and there was only a two-point increase in disapproval, to thirty-nine percent, with two percent expressing no opinion.

A Great Change

But the consistency existed only on the surface. There had been astonishing movement underneath. Almost a third of the respondents, thirty-one percent, changed positions. Half the time the change was slight, such as movement from approving somewhat to approving strongly. But for the other half, the second answer was different in kind. People who earlier said they approved Reagan's handling of the presidency were now saying they disapproved, and vice versa.

In all, sixteen percent of the people in the survey—a figure equivalent to more than twenty-five million citizens age eighteen or older—had thus changed their views on Reagan from positive to negative or the other way around in the course of a twenty- or twenty-five-minute telephone interview.

There were no loaded questions, no brainwashing, only references to a number of current issues. Had we wanted to lead people, we could probably have bounced Reagan's ratings up or down by ten points.

The lessons here are several. Many Americans have fragile political convictions; in late 1983, a time when Reagan was seen as being extremely popular, about one-third of the population could be said to have only superficial feelings about him, readily subject to change.

Sharp leadership debate by political opponents surely would have created such change. But most Democrats in Washington rarely showed interest in reaching out for such debate. Some supported Reagan; others remained silent, thereby abetting him. It was only in periods when the public led the way, such as in 1982, during the economic recession, and 1987, spurred by the calamitous revelations of Reagan's deceitful dealings with Iran and Nicaragua, that the opposition spoke up forcefully.

At other times, even in a debate format, Democrats tended to treat Reagan gently. . . .

82

Focusing on the bright side, national leaders have tried to keep the mass of Americans in the dark on serious issues, rarely explaining or even addressing them. The federal budget deficit first came into focus as a major concern only because Walter Mondale made it an election issue [in 1984]. Problems in race relations, never far beneath the consciousness of all Americans, were discussed only during periods of confrontation. Meanwhile, enrollment of blacks in the nation's colleges declined with hardly any notice.

For years, economic circumstances have forced mothers of young children to find jobs. That these women must return to work within weeks or a few months of giving birth is a national problem, not a sign of liberation.

The public perceives a national scandal in the lack of equity in the justice system. This country must find effective ways of dealing with crime and drugs, protecting the environment, restoring the infrastructure, making water sanitary, improving enormously expensive, frequently second-rate education, eliminating gross tax inequities, reducing unaffordable utility rates.

People care deeply about such issues; they would get involved if they were better informed and minimally encouraged. To quote Jefferson once more: "The people cannot be all, and always, well informed. The part which is wrong will be discontented, in proportion to the importance of the facts they misconceive. If they remain quiet under such misconceptions, it is a lethargy, a forerunner of death to the public liberty."

But leaders seldom take these problems to the people; their efforts go toward keeping the citizenry disengaged. The result, again as Jefferson envisioned it, in a letter written in 1788: "The natural progress of things is for liberty to yield and government to gain ground."

Most leaders look on the people with apprehension, many with contempt. The people recognize that, and they respond accordingly. . . .

Jefferson Understood the Problem

I would like to go back to the words of Thomas Jefferson cited earlier on the tension between government and public opinion in a democracy. On the one hand, as Jefferson put it, government degenerates when trusted to the rulers of the people alone. That maxim is terribly relevant today. As a nation, we may not be leaving our affairs totally to "the rulers," but we have gone a long way toward it. The result, more often than we would like, is a leadership whose goals are not those of the people, and whose methods—the only ones that could allow them to succeed—frequently include secrecy, demagoguery, and manipulation.

On the other hand, public opinion is most certainly as powerful now as it was when Jefferson called it an agitating force that "cannot be resisted," which is needed "to keep the waters pure." Public opinion almost invariably does have its way—once the people become aroused. Such was the lesson in the U.S. withdrawal from Vietnam, the resignation of Richard Nixon, the election defeat of Gerald Ford, and in the numerous, often dramatic, reversals of policy that Ronald Reagan was forced to make as president. But seldom does the public get aroused, or stay that way for long.

Leaders Are to Blame

Our leaders' practice of talking down to the public and avoiding true national debate has helped create a largely dulled citizenry, turning people away from public affairs and building in them resentment and distrust of government. One result is that where eighty percent of the people voted in presidential elections a hundred years ago, hardly more than half do so today.

This distrust and disengagement are the distinguishing features of Americans' views toward government and national politics, almost unchanged in the past fifteen or twenty years. In the end, citizenship is every individual's responsibility, and only so much blame may be laid to the political establishment. Nevertheless, the leaders' deliberate avoidance of true debate, the contempt they show the public during political campaigning, their use and refinement of propaganda techniques, the attentiveness of so many of them to moneyed interests and not to the people generally, all are major causes of the resentment and distrust.

Barry Sussman, *What Americans Really Think*, 1988.

In one sense, the thoughts of Jefferson are somewhat comforting. Governments have always tried to keep the people uninvolved and lethargic, and they always will; the present leaders' efforts are not a sign of some recent American collapse or decadence. "The natural progress of things," Jefferson wrote, "is for liberty to yield and government to gain ground." If he is right about that, today's relationship between government and the citizenry becomes more intelligible, part of the weave of history. If current leaders try to enact their own agenda rather than the public's—well, what else is new?

But to say a problem has always existed does not make it less real. When leaders substitute public relations for public debate, when officeholders, candidates, and political parties encourage stupor, and when, as a result, the public is ill-informed and distrustful, with almost half failing to vote—then, when all is said and done, it is just not satisfactory to accept that things have always been that way.

Under such circumstances it makes little sense to encourage wider public participation in public affairs; the "get-out-and-vote" cry every four years is misfounded. When people are unprepared to exercise sound judgment, they are easier to manipulate. Shrewd politicians may well create a democratic tyranny of the majority.

Jefferson's solution—to create an informed citizenry that can exert "control with a wholesome discretion"—is the correct one. But it is a goal that remains as distant today as it must have appeared then. And it will stay out of reach as long as leaders remain afraid of the people.

Creating an Informed Citizenry

After abandoning his race for the Democratic presidential nomination in February, 1988, Bruce Babbitt, the former governor of Arizona, laid out the problem in an article in the *Washington Post*. The candidates were all vague and "consensus-oriented," Babbitt wrote. As evidence, he cited their nonreaction to the continuing demonstrations by Palestinians in Israel—a matter of great urgency that American leaders, one would think, were obligated to address. "The Democrats had nothing to say about it," he wrote. (Neither, it may be added, did the Republicans at the time.) "Our process inhibits risk-taking," Babbitt said. "Part of it is the desire for a winner among our constituency groups. . . . They don't want us to emphasize any differences, stir any debate."

The public is not likely to develop a "wholesome discretion" unless the people at the top do stir up debate, and keep it stirred. There is no scarcity of good men and women among our national leaders, regardless of how things sometimes appear. Many of them frequently demonstrate personal and political courage, and act out of principle, not expediency. But almost all of them are terrified of public opinion.

Some intelligent leaders have always known that they are served best by openness, candor, and vigorous debate, not simply by creating an impression of openness and candor through platitudes and thirty-second advertisements. Candidates and those in power should get the message that real debate holds political rewards. Should that occur, there will be a lot of stirring and a more informed, participating citizenry. Progress may be slow, and clashes frequent. National problems will not disappear or be easily resolved. But a genuine respect for government would emerge, and we could say, legitimately, that it is morning in America.

"*Recommendations to revitalize political parties . . . represent a continuation of the historical struggle to realize democracy in the United States.*"

Reinvigorate Political Parties

John J. Kushma

In the nineteenth century, political parties provided a strong link between citizens and the government. In the following viewpoint, John J. Kushma argues that this is no longer the case. He states that this alienation between the parties and citizens has caused many people to abandon their parties. Simultaneously, however, grassroots organizations such as consumer and environmental groups have grown in number and strength. Kushma believes that political parties should tap into this renewed activism and use this interest to strengthen their parties and thereby increase voter participation. Kushma is a writer, editor, and historian who has taught history at the University of Texas at Arlington.

As you read, consider the following questions:

1. Why does the author believe that U.S. democracy is undergoing a slow and protracted death?
2. What specific reforms does Kushma advocate to reinvigorate local political parties?
3. How would Kushma reform America's elections?

John J. Kushma, "Participation and the Democratic Agenda: Theory and Praxis." Reprinted from *The State and Democracy: Revitalizing America's Government*, edited by Mark V. Levine et al., by permission of the publisher, Routledge, Chapman and Hall, Inc.

The decline of electoral participation, the slow decomposition of legislative parties, the lack of coherence between the executive branch and Congress, and the partisan dealignment of the electorate all testify to the weakness of what have traditionally been the predominant agencies of democratic politics. To the extent that fewer voters go to the polls and our political parties continue to deteriorate, we face more than a crisis of political performance. U.S. democracy is undergoing a slow and protracted death. Should an economic collapse or an equally devastating national crisis occur, the weakness of the agencies of democratic governance will be quickly apparent, for it is unlikely that such a crisis would be resolved in a democratic manner.

Elections, Parties, and Democracy

One entrenched principle of democracy, for example, is the belief that elections ought to ensure public control over governmental leaders and public policy or at least institutionalize the responsiveness of the state to public opinion. Building on inherited British wisdom, the American revolutionary generation viewed elections as an important means for protecting citizens from the arbitrary exercise of power by governmental leaders.

Equally important to the democratic tradition, though less frequently articulated, is the recognition that elections legitimate and strengthen the state and mobilize popular support for the regime. James Wilson, more democratically inclined than the majority of delegates to the Constitutional Convention, nonetheless joined with conservatives in favoring a strong national government; he understood that a strong national government required popular participation. Wilson proclaimed himself in favor of "raising the federal pyramid to a considerable altitude, and for that reason wished to give it as broad a base as possible," through popular elections. Other delegates reluctantly endorsed the popular election of representatives because they could see no alternative. They knew that Americans would never accept a government that did not secure its legitimacy and power through elections. As the avowedly elitist George Mason admonished his colleagues, "Notwithstanding the oppressions and injustices experienced among us from democracy, the genius of the people is in favor of it, and the genius of the people must be consulted."

Despite the widespread antipathy to political parties in the late eighteenth century and the "constitution against parties" drafted by the Constitutional Convention, political parties emerged as those agencies through which Americans would realize the potential for popular control and mobilization of public support. It is appropriate that . . . the American people and government revert to their first principles and recognize that democracy demands an active citizenry. Democracy requires popular participation in an electoral process that ensures the state legitimacy and authority to realize the humane, just, and equitable society the American people desire. . . .

This analysis also suggests a resolution to the paradox of political participation in the United States and an explanation for the deterioration of political parties. Americans have realized that these traditional agencies of democracy no longer function as effectively to mediate between citizens and the state. Many people have consequently abandoned them or have continued to participate in them in a more or less ritualistic manner. To the extent that they have done so, democracy has been weakened. To the extent that they increasingly continue to do so, democracy is at risk. . . .

The New Populism

Yet, there are signs that the "new populism" across the country—citizen action groups, consumer groups, neighborhood associations, the environmental movement—represents a return to democratic traditions. Less vocal and strident than the new left of the 1960s, the new populism is also more rooted in real as opposed to visionary communities where practical experience in democracy is available and the concepts of democratic citizenship and equality are more existentially meaningful. The movement's growth has been impressive, and its potential to revitalize the American political system is genuine.

Strong Political Parties Make Elections Relevant

Generally speaking, strong party organizations enhance the significance of elections, while declines in party strength reduce the importance of electoral processes. Inasmuch as their influence derives from the electoral arena, political parties are the institutions with the largest stake in upholding the principle that power should be allocated through elections. Thus, a diminution of party influence and an increase in the power of other political agencies is likely not only to reduce the relevance of elections for governmental programs and policies but also to allow electoral results themselves to be circumvented, resisted, or even reversed by forces that control powerful institutions outside the electoral realm.

Benjamin Ginsberg and Martin Shefter, *Politics by Other Means*, 1990.

Even in the face of these hopeful signs, however, the decomposition of parties and the decline in electoral turnout continue. Clearly, something more than community-based organizing is needed to reconstruct a democratic political system. The deterioration of the channels linking citizens and the state suggests that the solution must comprehend the larger structures of mediation in U.S. politics. . . .

The solution is not simply to find the most appropriate and appealing policies. In many respects political parties are more concerned with and have more policymaking structures than ever. The problem is not how to organize parties more effectively at the national level; today's parties have created truly integrated national organizations, especially the Republicans. Rather, what was traditionally the heart of the vibrant nineteenth-century American political parties—the local party—is dying. Lacking in organizational vitality and resources, overwhelmed by candidates and their independent committees, robbed of many of its functions by professional consultants, the local party no longer functions as a participatory and deliberative organization. The success of the numerically small Lyndon LaRouche forces in taking over the local Democratic organizations and of the new right in Republican local party organizations is proof. . . .

New Populists Must Work Through Parties

Unfortunately, many of the organizations that comprise the new populist movement have ignored or actively avoided electoral and partisan activity, considering alliances beyond the bounds of their local communities threatening to their integrity and authenticity. (The Citizens Party is, of course, a notable exception.) Consequently, there has been no concerted challenge to the dominance of capital, the powerful, entrenched organizations, and the national policies that facilitate the anti-democratic aspects of communal economic and social life on a national scale. The new populism has failed to realize its inherent potential to spark authentic American democracy.

Transforming the new populism into a national political movement with the potential to revitalize American democracy will not be easily accomplished, for the new populists' commitment to the local community is deeply entrenched. . . .

Yet, unless these local new populist movements extend beyond the bounds of their communities, they will ultimately retreat into sectarianism and defensiveness and hence fail to recognize the similarity of interests and ideas they potentially share with millions of other U.S. citizens. Likewise, unless these fragmented movements coalesce and challenge the entrenched interests that corrupt the national polity as well as the local community, the undemocratic structures of power in this country will remain fundamentally unchanged, despite their heroic efforts.

A democratic reinvigoration of local partisan politics would allow community-based democratic movements to employ the traditional channels of democratic mediation in the United States without fear of losing their authenticity. In order for this to happen, the new populist movements together with traditional reform constituencies like organized labor, must actively undertake to change both the structure and operation of local parties.

Recent changes in national party rules, court decisions, and governmental policies have conspired to weaken local parties and political parties in general. Although some of these changes have emerged from laudable motives, a thorough reform of party organization and operation is needed in order to transform political parties into more authentic agencies of democratic mediation.

Transforming the Parties

Parties have ceased to be deliberative organizations at all levels, particularly with respect to candidate selection, an area in need of tremendous reform. Parties must offer citizens more than simply the opportunity to cast votes in primary elections. Insofar as possible, caucuses and conventions should replace primary elections so that education and conflict resolution can assume their rightful roles in the political process.

Local parties should play a major role in their own revitalization by promoting voter registration and educational programs. Parties should be encouraged to develop a concept of party membership, defined by the payment of nominal dues. Party decisions and activities should be limited to party members. Where party registration is not provided in state law, legislative action will be necessary to restrict participation in party primaries to party registrants. Where primaries are retained in state law, these laws should be amended to provide for party endorsement of candidates. Above all, local parties must be popular democratic organizations with their own autonomy.

Party organizations should be adequately funded by a dues-paying membership, supplemented by federal matching funds in whatever multiples are necessary. (Public opinion polls strongly suggest that abstention from voting is a consequence of the belief that all candidates are so mortgaged to special interests that it matters little who wins.) Qualifications for public funds for parties should be established at the local level so that local community groups can organize themselves into a party for local elections. Up to a certain level tax credits should be given for contributions to parties and eliminated for contributions to political action committees or candidates to help institutionalize collective partisan responsibility. Campaign finance reform has generally weakened parties by focussing on candidates rather than on parties, thereby reinforcing candidate fundraising and organization at the expense of party influence. It has similarly weakened parties vis-à-vis interest groups. This imbalance needs to be redressed. . . .

Local elections should be returned to a partisan basis not only to strengthen local party organization but also to provide more linkage between local and national politics. This would put a premium on more human-scale, face-to-face politics and provide more incentives for participating in local party activities. It would also encourage local parties to take more initiative in scheduling policy forums and debates. Much new communications technology, including interactive cable television, provides a fruitful opportunity for local political groups and should be explored as well.

Parties Have Lost Out to Interest Groups

In this country, our parties can no longer punch their way out of a paper sack. When I was first elected, the most powerful political forces in my state were the Democrats and the Republicans. Now, they are the Minnesotans for Life, the AFL-CIO and the National Education Association. They have legitimate claims on the process, but all of them operate under a much smaller umbrella than the parties.

Bill Frenzel, *The Washington Post National Weekly Edition*, May 14-May 20, 1990.

The above recommendations should partially answer some of the concerns that groups comprising the new populist movement have about participating in electoral politics. My goal here is not to suggest a tactical alliance with any existing partisan organization but to offer ideas about how the structure and operation of parties can be altered so that they pose no threat to community groups and in fact enhance the possibilities for democratic politics. The appropriate and effective vehicle for the new populists can be a third party (assuming existing barriers to a place on the ballot and public funding are reduced to an appropriate level), the local Democratic Party, or a caucus within the local Democratic Party. The choice should be dictated by community traditions and prevailing political forces.

Changes in Conduct of Elections

Finally, a number of changes in the conduct of elections would facilitate their reemergence as agencies of democratic mediation. Some, discussed briefly below, would be easy to realize. We must begin by recognizing that placing *any* burden on the exercise of the franchise is undemocratic. We do not know exactly the degree to which current registration procedures inhibit participation, but it is clear that they do nothing to encourage citizens to exercise their voting rights. The state already keeps track of citizens in a variety of ways, from federal and state tax lists to the Census. Universal, state-sponsored registration should be encouraged. As a temporary and expedient alternative, election day registration should immediately become law.

Lack of information inhibits participation in elections. The state should assume responsibility for providing information about elections, both partisan and referenda. Something like the Oregon pamphlet system (in which candidates are provided with free space in a publication that is made available to all voters) should be applied to all elections. Free time for candidates and parties on commercial and public radio and television stations should also be allocated.

Two-Day Elections

Finally, to facilitate both individual voting and local party volunteer activity, two-day elections should become the norm. A shift to weekend elections would also provide local and community-based organizations the opportunity to play a more important role in mobilizing citizens.

The above recommendations seem to pale in comparison to the contemporary political crisis. But these practical recommendations to revitalize political parties, simplify voting, facilitate new forms of political organization, and encourage greater citizen participation in electoral politics are in fact radical. They represent a continuation of the historical struggle to realize democracy in the United States.

"Higher turnout may well depend on long-term rebuilding of American communities."

Rebuild America's Communities

Gerald M. Pomper and Loretta A. Sernekos

Gerald M. Pomper is a professor of political science at Rutgers University in New Brunswick, New Jersey, where Loretta A. Sernekos is a doctoral candidate in political science. In the following viewpoint, Pomper and Sernekos argue that people who feel a strong sense of attachment to their local communities are more likely to vote than people who feel only a modest attachment to their communities. Unfortunately, the authors continue, the overall strength of America's communities has declined in recent years because of increased mobility and other social factors. Since declining voter turnout parallels the decline of America's communities, the authors conclude that rebuilding those communities is crucial to increasing turnout.

As you read, consider the following questions:

1. What do the authors mean by the "bake sale" theory of voter participation?
2. What five individual attitudes concerning political participation were studied by Pomper and Sernekos?

Excerpted from "Bake Sales and Voting" by Gerald M. Pomper and Loretta A. Sernekos, *Society*, July/August 1991. Reprinted with permission.

In the town where we live, bake sales are held at the polls on election day and voting turnout is generally high. Waiting to vote one year, we thought that there might be a connection, that bake sales might stimulate higher turnout. Hence, the "bake sale" theory of voting participation.

More precisely, the bake sale theory holds that voting participation, beyond all other factors, will be higher among persons who are more fully integrated into their communities, finding satisfaction in the community life. Most explanations of voting patterns are incomplete, because they rest on individualistic, even atomistic, assumptions. A full explanation must place the individual voting behavior within a social context. It must, as our metaphor suggests, take note of the bake sale as well as the voting booth.

Voters decide to pay the cost of balloting because of certain individual characteristics, such as formal education and campaign interest. However, individualistic explanations are incomplete. As they decide to participate, voters pay little attention to utilitarian, policy-based differences among the parties. Rather, they consider more general attitudes toward politics.

People who vote are also likely to be people who patronize bake sales. In both cases, the expected benefits may be very small and the costs are irrelevant. Both acts are expressions of community solidarity, a sharing and a ritual. Citizens who make a personal commitment to their local, interpersonal communities make the same kind of commitment when they vote. Voters are not so much atomistic calculators of personal advantage as they are citizens. Or, to invoke Lazarsfeld's famous phrase: "A person thinks [and acts] politically, as he is, socially."

In the last two decades, considerable attention, and anxiety, has been directed both to the relatively low turnout in America, as compared to other democracies, and to the decline in turnout since the 1960 presidential election. As early as 1960, E. E. Schattschneider described the limited American electorate as a "broadly-based oligarchy." Some analysts have criticized the social-class biases of voting, as participation at the polls continues to decline, while others have sought to explain this trend as both anomalous and ominous. . . .

Psychological Explanations

For the current study, five individual attitudes were examined: strength of partisanship, external efficacy, internal efficacy, interest in the campaign, and citizen duty. It stands to reason that people are more likely to vote if they are strongly committed to a political party, if they find the world of politics responsive, understandable, and interesting, and if they accept the conventional civic obligation to vote. These attitudes are partially individualistic. Unlike demographic characteristics, however, they are more subject to change within social contexts.

A sense of citizen duty seems to be particularly important. Indeed, in a major elaboration of Downsian theory, William Riker and Peter Ordeshook found the civic rewards of voting to be a major explanation of turnout. Even earlier, *The American Voter* found turnout to be markedly affected by the sense of citizen duty, although this attitude was itself strongly dependent on level of education.

All of these attitudes showed consistent, though varied, relationships to turnout in the elections of 1984 and 1988. These attitudes were also found to be helpful in explaining a notable decline in strong partisanship during this period, as well as a decided decline in external efficacy and a possible decline in citizen duty. . . . Measuring the impact of two of these factors—partisanship and external efficacy—Ruy Teixeira found that they accounted for 38 percent of the drop in turnout from 1960 to 1980. Conversely, he found these two factors accounted for 46 percent of the increase in turnout between 1980 to 1984. Still, the puzzle is not completely solved. We need to look beyond these individualistic causes.

Voting turnout is affected by demographic characteristics, by rational calculations of the potential effects of the vote on individual voters, and by attitudes toward politics. If we confined our attention to such factors, we could imagine that people cast votes in private, much as they choose their television programs, and analysis of turnout would be similar to Nielsen surveys.

These explanations, however, leave something out; they leave out the local flavor of an election and its social character. Contrast this image of isolated voting to that conveyed by Tocqueville's description of American politics in an earlier period:

> As the election draws near, the activity of intrigue and the agitation of the populace increase; the citizens are divided into hostile camps, each of which assumes the name of its favorite candidate; the whole nation glows with feverish excitement; the election is the daily theme of the press, the subject of private conversations, the end of every thought and every action, the sole interest of the present.

This description suggests an historical parallel between the high turnouts of the nineteenth century and the closer community life of that period. Urban machines brought voters to the polls not only because voters were paid for their ballots, but because voting was an expression of the voters' integration into a local, typically ethnic, network of personal associations. . . .

Effect of Bake Sales

Our focus is the integration of voters into their communities. This integration is posited as close face-to-face relationships in three contexts: the family, the residential community, and peer groups. Family, residence, and group affiliations are viewed as different aspects of the social connectedness of individuals, as some of the ways in which they separate themselves from the "lonely crowd," and become part of active political networks.

Participation Can Create Civic Responsibility

As citizens are afforded more meaningful participation in public decision making and ·as more effective avenues of public intervention are created, citizens will be encouraged to invest time and energy in acquiring political information and skills. Similarly, effective and meaningful participation in public decisions will, we believe, inculcate and nurture authentic democratic values and a sense of civic and social responsibility.

John J. Kushma, *The State and Democracy*, 1988.

To test the relationship of community integration to turnout, we employ eight "bake sale" variables that provide reasonably appropriate measures of integration into individuals' immediate social milieu, and of their commitment to their communities. . . . The first variable—being married—represents a personal commitment to the small community of the family. We expect higher turnout among married people. . . . Three other variables represent commitment to the residential community. We expect higher turnout among persons who own, rather than rent, their homes; who have lived longer in their current town or city; and who have lived longer in their current specific home. The final four variables represent commitment to group communities. We expect higher turnout among persons who are more frequent churchgoers; who come from families with union members; who discuss politics frequently; and who belong to or take part in formal organizations of those people to whom they feel "closest" (for example, a religious group for those who feel closest to their coreligionists). . . .

[After testing our theory using turnout data from 1984 and 1988, we found that] community participation is an important independent factor. . . . Turnout is considerably more likely among people who are regular churchgoers, who are members of organizations, political discussants, homeowners, and who are long-time residents in the same home, regardless of demography. . . .

Reformulating Explanations of Turnout

To explain turnout, social context must be included in a theory broadened beyond individualistic explanations. . . . The social benefits accruing to voters include the psychological satisfaction of performing a prescribed duty of citizens, an enhanced reputation for political awareness, and the attention received from party workers and candidates seeking support from the voter.

A social perspective also provides a better understanding of the effect of costs on turnout. For a particular voter weighing individualistic benefits and costs rationally, the infinitesimal policy benefits of voting can never equal the real and significant costs. To understand why voters bear these costs, we need to see how apparent costs become converted into benefits. Corruption is one means of conversion, to take an egregious example. In the past, when political machines bought votes, they relieved the voters of the costs of acquiring information (and, sometimes, even of the physical strain of marking a ballot). They converted the cost of the voter's time into the direct personal benefit of a cash payment or a drink, as well as, not infrequently, the psychological benefits of good fellowship and ethnic solidarity.

More honest conversion takes place in a social context. The cost of driving to the polls and spending time voting converts into the benefit of greeting friends and neighbors. Just as we pay these costs without noticing when we go out to dinner, voters pay them at the polls (especially if there is a bake sale). Notice how often people remain at the polls after voting, exchanging news and gossip. If time were a cost, they would leave immediately and avoid further losses. But if time spent with neighbors is a benefit, then their slow departure is rational.

In similar fashion, the cost of casting a ballot is converted into the benefit of identifying oneself with the constituency, local or national. This identification is fostered by patriotic symbols at the polls, such as the flag. Again, the cost of political information can be seen as a benefit because it facilitates interpersonal communication, providing another topic for conversation beyond the weather and sports.

Increasing Voter Turnout

Previous analysis emphasized individual costs, particularly the ways in which rational voters could reduce their information costs by shifting them to others, or employing "free" information. These conclusions can also be recast into a social perspective. It is well known, for example, that turnout increases when political parties make deliberate efforts to mobilize the vote. This is usually explained in terms of reduced individual cost of information. However, it can also be seen as establishing new social ties between the canvasser and the voter by drawing the new voter into an expanded political community. Given the low information content of most campaign literature, the latter explanation may be more accurate. . . .

A long-term increase in turnout will require both a broadened theory of participation and extensive social change. Political scientists can make some contribution to the first requirement. Theories of voting have been essentially atomistic, even Hobbesian, focusing on isolated individuals, calculating their utilitarian advantages in a psychological state of nature, their attention to politics only "solitary, poor, nasty, brutish, and short."

We might do better to return to the Aristotelian premise that humans are by nature social and political animals. If we think of voting as a community act, we might see it as a manifestation, or vestige, of a different polity, "a democracy based on friendship." There, as Jane Mansbridge suggests: "Participants are equal in status; the costs of participation, of which some make so much, do not feel heavy. Citizens 'fly to the assemblies' as if to meet their friends. They value the time they spend on their common affairs."

From this premise, we can speculate that community involvement explains the trends in voter participation. The past quarter of a century has evidenced a continuation, perhaps an acceleration, of the historical decline of American communities. Robert Bellah illustrates the change in his description of the contemporary life of a "traditional" New England town:

> Three-fourths of Suffolk's present population have moved in within the past twenty-five years. . . . If five hundred out of the town's nine thousand registered voters show up for a town meeting, that is considered a very good turnout. . . . They live, in Suffolk because it happens to be conveniently located for them and the housing prices there happen to fit their budgets. . . . They probably looked on the town's anniversary celebration as a set of quaint festivities—pleasant diversions for a weekend afternoon, not rituals expressing something important about the meaning of their lives.

The change in this one community is not unique. The more general decline of communities in American life not only parallels, but is a cause of the decline in voter turnout. Indicators of these social changes match our community integration variables. They can be found in a higher divorce rate and lower birth rates, increased residential mobility, the disappearance of three-generation residential families, the replacement of interpersonal communication by mass media, the transformation of interest groups into professional entrepreneurships, and the replacement of local, interpersonal political party organizations with impersonal, national party bureaucracies run by campaign consultants. . . .

The Importance of Rebuilding Communities

The importance of community integration for voter turnout has serious implications for likely future trends and for deliberate reform efforts. The changes in American life, the waning of bake sales, if you will, are not simply changes in taste, but they are the effects of essentially irreversible changes in the economy, demographic structure, and gender roles. These effects cannot be reversed by simple exhortations of citizen duty, especially in an era when most Americans no longer have an intense personal understanding of the requirements of citizenship. . . .

Community Involvement vs. Individual Pursuit

If thinking of ourselves as members of a community made us poorer, there would still be reasons to advocate it; but the fact is that commitment to a community turns out to be a much stronger basis for an effective economy than the individual pursuit of self-interest. We have only to look at the case of Japan to see that. . . .

The question is not just what should government do but how it can do it in a way that strengthens the initiative and participation of citizens, both as individuals and within their communities and associations, rather than reducing them to the status of clients.

Robert Bellah, *The Good Society*, 1991.

Institutional barriers can certainly be lowered further, most obviously by easing re-registration upon a change of residence or most radically by substituting state-directed for personal registration. There is a limit to institutional change, however. . . .

Ultimately, higher turnout may well depend on long-term rebuilding of American communities—a difficult task, and perhaps an impossible one. To achieve a higher vote, public policy must be directed not simply toward easier individual registration, but also toward strengthening local civic life through family stability, neighborhood empowerment, participatory interest groups, and active political parties. It may be well to remember Tocqueville's warning that individualism ultimately undermines social cohesion and leads to an electorate, however large, that is but "an innumerable multitude of men, all equal and alike, incessantly endeavoring to procure the petty and paltry pleasures with which they glut their lives." In such a community, each individual is, in Tocqueville's words, "living apart, as a stranger to the fate of all the rest—his children and his friends constitute to him the whole of mankind; as for the rest of his fellow-citizens, he is close to them, but he sees them not; he touches them, but he feels them not; he exists but in himself and for himself alone; and if his kindred still remain to him, he may be said at any rate to have lost his country."

"Our nation must ask our young people to participate and show them how they can."

Educate Youth in Citizenship

People for the American Way

People for the American Way is a nonpartisan organization committed to reaffirming the traditional American values of tolerance, pluralism, and freedom of expression and religion. The organization is deeply concerned about low participation in American elections, and works to increase voter turnout. In the following viewpoint, the author presents the results of a survey that examined the political involvement and attitudes of young Americans. The survey's results reveal that young Americans are very apathetic about politics. If families, schools, and government leaders set a positive example for America's youth and encourage them to get involved, political participation will increase, the author concludes.

As you read, consider the following questions:

1. What evidence does the author present to support the belief that young Americans are apathetic about politics and civic involvement?
2. According to the author, how have families, schools, and government let young people down?

Excerpted from *Democracy's Next Generation: A Study of Youth and Teachers* by People for the American Way, Washington, DC, 1989.

Today's young Americans are tomorrow's stewards of our democracy. Only an informed, involved citizenry will be able to steer our nation into a new century, meeting complex challenges ranging from illiteracy to global warming. If indeed eternal vigilance is the price of liberty, then the next generation of Americans must be ready when their time comes to take up the watch.

But we cannot expect our young people to be better citizens than the adults around them. Today, an ever-increasing number of Americans are reluctant to exercise even the most basic responsibilities of citizenship. Voter turnout in the 1988 election reached its lowest ebb in more than half a century. Political leaders, analysts and the media warn us that we are witnessing a disturbing slide toward apathy and disengagement from the political process.

If we are to reverse this dangerous trend, we must strengthen the civic values and expand the civic participation of democracy's next generation. People For the American Way commissioned a study to examine our youth's understanding of and commitment to three important aspects of citizenship in a democracy: meeting personal responsibilities, serving the community, and participating in the nation's political life.

Conducted for People For the American Way by Peter D. Hart Research Associates, the study assesses young people's views of such topics as personal values and aspirations, community service, politics, images of America, concepts of citizenship, and influences on their notions of citizenship and civic involvement. Social studies teachers were also interviewed, on the assumption that they shoulder the major responsibility for citizenship education in our schools. The study has four components: telephone surveys with 1006 young people (ages 15-24); in-depth one-on-one interviews with another group of 100 youth; a second telephone survey of 405 social studies teachers, and focus group interviews with teachers conducted in Providence, Rhode Island and Kansas City, Missouri. . . .

Democracy's Next Generation

A snapshot of young America today captures a group in transition. The young people surveyed, who range in age from 15 to 24 years old and come from widely varied socioeconomic backgrounds, are moving gradually toward the full assumption of adult responsibilities. Most are just beginning to awaken to the larger political world of ideas and decision making outside their homes, schools and neighborhoods. Many face financial or family stresses that inhibit their ability to become more active in their communities.

Even in the best of circumstances, young people face a difficult transition into full participation in our democracy. Our findings indicate that—due in large part to the failure of adult society to instill strong citizenship values and inspire involvement—today's young Americans are ill-prepared to accept this responsibility.

The nation's youth clearly appreciate the democratic freedoms that, they say, make theirs the "best country in the world to live in." Asked to describe in their own words what makes America special, 63 percent named the rights and freedoms our citizens enjoy. Like all young people, they are enchanted by "the freedom to do as we please when we please," in the words of one respondent.

But young people fail to grasp the other half of the democratic equation: the responsibility to participate in the hard work of self-government. This incomplete understanding emerged vividly when young people were asked to describe a "good citizen." To them, the task of being a good citizen carries no additional meaning or special responsibilities beyond simply being a "good person": one who helps people in need or is generous or caring. "Honest, good friend, trustworthy" was one typical characterization. Remarkably, only 12 percent of the youth surveyed linked citizenship to one basic duty of self-government: voting.

Today's Young People Are Less Involved

This is a generation overwhelmingly preoccupied with events within their personal sphere. Asked to assign a rank to their life goals on a scale of one to ten, 72 percent gave a nine or a ten to career success, 68 percent to having a close-knit family life, and 57 percent to enjoying life and having a good time. Being involved in helping the community to be a better place ranked dead last, chosen as a priority by only 24 percent.

Young people say they feel too pressured by the demands in their personal lives to get involved in civic activities. Fifty-three percent blame demands such as "getting good grades or getting a good job" for their lack of involvement. Teachers acknowledge that many young people are grappling with genuine stresses such as family problems or economic hardship. "Kids today, some of them are really trying to cope, just to cope," observed one teacher. But youth's focus on the personal is sometimes seen as less legitimate: "My kids are going to look at [community involvement] and say, 'Well, that's not going to buy me a Gucci shirt . . . what's in it for me?'" another teacher commented.

Personal concerns appear to eclipse any significant attention to the political life of our nation. By 45 to 21 percent, teachers see today's high school students as less interested in politics and public affairs than their counterparts a decade ago. "A very small percentage of them care, and a very small percentage are interested," according to a teacher. "The others think it is boring, boring, boring." Only 16 percent of youth report having a "great deal" of interest in current events, politics and government.

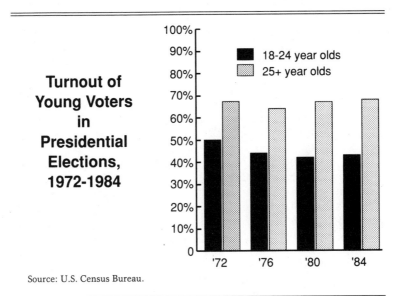

Turnout of Young Voters in Presidential Elections, 1972-1984

18-24 year olds
25+ year olds

'72   '76   '80   '84

Source: U.S. Census Bureau.

Boredom and apathy are also reflected in dwindling civic involvement. Three-fourths of young people agree strongly or slightly with the statement that "young people seem less involved these days than they were in the past." Forty-six percent of social studies teachers say that the students in their classrooms today are less active and involved than those of ten years ago.

The disconnection young people apparently feel between their own lives and the life of the nation becomes especially telling when they are asked to think about the future. While a strong majority are confident about their own personal prospects, only 42 percent said they feel optimistic about America's future, with a narrow plurality—47 percent—stating that they are worried that America's best years might be behind us. This generation seems unaware that the fate of the nation is intertwined with their own individual destinies.

We Have Let Young People Down

Young people look to their parents as by far the most important influence on the development of their civic values. But the evidence suggests that parents often fail to deliver on these expectations. Eighty-four percent of teachers cite lack of parental encouragement as a major reason for the non-involvement of youth. As one teacher summed up this point, "If parents don't have time to deal with the Girl Scouts or the heart campaign or politicking in the community or cleaning up their neighborhood, the kids won't." Nearly half of young people also highlight this cause of their non-involvement.

Schools—another key source of citizenship preparation—get mixed grades. Forty-three percent of young people cite schools' inadequacies as a major cause of their lack of community involvement. While school is the leading source of community service options for those youth who are active, only 20 percent of teachers characterize their school's commitment to community service as "very strong." Only half say their school has a voter registration program that "aggressively tries to register eligible students."

Political leaders are not only failing to impart citizenship values, they are actually alienating young people from public life. Fifty-four percent of teachers cite the poor example set by politicians as a strong reason for youth's non-involvement. Most young people (53 percent) think that they can trust the government in Washington to do what's right only "some" or "none" of the time. As one young woman put it, "There's been so much scandal and so much sleaze and fraud going on in the government today. . . . You get to the point where you think that it's not worth being involved in, and that all politicians are corrupt, so why be involved in it?"

Young People Have the Answers

America's youth have an abundance of good intentions. Overwhelmingly, they describe themselves as "likely" to engage in such activities as helping an elderly neighbor or working an hour a week on a community project. By 58 percent to 38 percent, today's youth reject the notion that "people should take care of themselves and shouldn't expect others to do things for them."

They strongly support the idea of community service. Fifty-one percent think that such service should be a high-school graduation requirement, and an even larger proportion (89 percent) suggest that volunteering for such service be rewarded with school credit. Both teachers and students argue for a more hands-on, participatory approach to teaching about citizenship, and they say this should start at an early age. One young man, active in his community, explains: "As soon as you turn eighteen, it's not like you can just switch on our 'vote' modes and go out and vote. I think if we were encouraged to be involved earlier on, then we'd definitely have a bigger [showing]."

Those young people who have gotten involved in community service provide a clear illustration of youth's potential. A sizable

minority (38 percent) of our young people report having per-
formed some type of community or neighborhood service
within the past year.

Dismal Statistics

We must develop a new public-private partnership to help citizens register, vote, and participate in democracy. Schools and
businesses—which have done all too little to encourage voting—
must join with community organizations to begin to turn the dismal voting statistics around.

Arthur J. Kropp, People for the American Way *Newsletter*, October 21, 1988.

Within this group are some exceptional young people who provide a profile of active, engaged youth. . . . Those who serve
strengthen their ties to the community, gain a broader sense of
their responsibilities, and—perhaps most important—get a taste
of the rewards of participation.

Craig, a college student in Spartanburg, South Carolina, has
worked on a range of projects from helping the homeless to environmental cleanup activities. He is critical of the job schools
and government leaders have done in encouraging youth involvement. He says the message youth need to hear is that "the
services they're going to get involved in are worthwhile, and the
people will appreciate it more than they can imagine."

The example set by her grandfather's community involvement
inspired 16-year-old Jill of Independence, Missouri, to follow his
lead. She has done volunteer work for the elderly and environmental causes, and the satisfaction she gets from this work
keeps her active and involved. "I really like to help people," she
says.

More young people can be stirred from disengagement to action if society makes this a priority mission. The message of this
study's results is clear: our nation must ask our young people to
participate and show them how they can.

Shaping Good Citizens

Our nation can only expect democracy's next generation to be
prepared to assume their citizenship responsibilities if adult society does its part to get them ready. We need a top-to-bottom
rekindling of America's special commitment: to one another and
to our democratic system. While remaining realistic about the
limitations and barriers facing many of your youth, our society
must try harder to ensure that young Americans:

• Understand that their rights as citizens of this democracy
carry with them accompanying responsibilities.

- Are registered to vote, if eligible, and aware of how and where to exercise this right.
- Participate in a service project as a requirement for high school graduation.
- Are well informed about how democracy works, the many avenues of citizen participation in a democratic system, and the major issues confronting our nation.

Helping our young people to develop a citizenship ethic and sense of responsibility to one another will take a team effort. Therefore, we issue this challenge to those who have the most power to effect improvements.

A Challenge

- A Challenge to All Eligible Citizens: to register and vote. There could be no stronger positive signal to young people than a surge in voter participation during the 1990s.
- A Challenge to Parents: to create a "culture of citizenship" in each household by voting, keeping informed about public affairs, participating in community activities, and sharing these experiences with children. Parents serve as important "citizen role models" for their children, just as they are models as family heads and breadwinners. Children can begin to learn the importance of involvement at home, by being assigned regular responsibilities appropriate to their ages and participating in family-initiated service projects in their neighborhoods.
- A Challenge to Schools: to restore an emphasis on their earliest traditional mission—the preparation of informed citizens capable of self-government. Schools should develop more community service opportunities, building on the good programs already available and making sure these are fully integrated into the curriculum. Schools should focus on participatory approaches to teaching youth about citizenship, including providing a forum for the debate of public issues. And, finally, schools should see that all eligible students are registered to vote by the time they graduate.
- A Challenge to Political Leaders: to set an example of leadership for young people, to spend time with them and listen to their concerns, and to make an active effort to encourage their involvement in public life. . . .
- A Challenge to Young Americans: to recognize that the freedoms they cherish depend on their readiness to assume the stewardship of our democracy. While adults must do more to open avenues of involvement for youth, young people must be prepared to meet them halfway. In the words of one young American in this survey, "the community is theirs and they should work for it; that's why they should get involved."

106

"Low voter turnout is a leading indicator of contentment."

Low Voter Participation Is Not a Problem

Charles Krauthammer

In recent years many political analysts have bemoaned America's low voter turnout. Such analysts believe low turnout signifies voter apathy and a disinterest in government and politics. In the following viewpoint, Charles Krauthammer states that, while it is true that Americans are uninterested in politics, this lack of interest is a positive, not a negative, sign. People participate in politics when they are unhappy and seek change, Krauthammer contends. Low voter turnout is simply a sign that Americans are content. Krauthammer is a well-known columnist for periodicals such as *The New Republic* and *Time*, and the author of several books.

As you read, consider the following questions:

1. What does Krauthammer mean when he refers to the "marginalization of Washington"?
2. Why is Krauthammer relieved that politics is declining in importance?
3. What is the benefit of being indifferent to politics, in the author's opinion?

Washington, it seems, is a city in decline. History has taken up residence in Budapest and Tokyo, Brussels and Seoul. After a brief spurt of prominence and wealth owed to the Depression, Hitler and the cold war, Washington, we are told, has lapsed into a somnambular state.

This is an exaggeration, but not too far from the truth. Government has grown huge, and a presidential hiccup can still panic the stock market, but Washington has far less impact on the direction of America and the world than it did a generation ago.

The marginalization of Washington is sometimes taken as proof of American decline. Nonsense. With the implosion of its only superpower rival, America stands alone in the world, its relative power—which the decline theorists insist is the only relevant measure—unsurpassed. (One reason, for example, that hostages are being released is that the thug regimes of the world realize that suddenly there is only one superpower left and they had better warm up to it.)

The Decline of Politics

The marginalization of Washington reflects not the decline of America but the decline of politics. In the West—and it is soon to be true in the East, now that they've got the easy part, revolution, out of the way—history is not made by politics. It is made by economics, by demographics and, above all, by science and technology. Politics lubricates, corrupts mildly and takes a slice of the action. But it does not create new worlds as it did, horribly, in 1917 and 1933 and, blessedly, in 1946-49 when the U.S. established the structures of the postwar world. Politics has become, like much of life, maintenance. The house is built; Republicans and Democrats argue now over who is to repair the roof and how to pay for it.

Moreover, the great political debates are over. The romance with isms, with the secular religions of socialism, egalitarianism and totalitarianism, is dead. The fierce battles over whether, for example, the U.S. should lead the crusade against communism are finished too. American politics is no longer about bearing any burden in defense of liberty. American politics is about the Clean Air Act.

This is not to deride clean air. Clean air is important, and the clean air bill now working its way through Congress is a quite satisfying triumph of democratic compromise, smog-producing Detroit working out with smog-ingesting Los Angeles a political arrangement that the whole country can live with. But the great dichotomies of war and peace, left and right, good and evil are gone. Politicians still try to use these categories to carry the fight, but no one believes them.

This triumph of apolitical bourgeois democracy has been a

source of dismay to some. They pine for the heroic age when great ideologies clashed and the life of nations turned on a vote in Congress. On the contrary. I couldn't be happier that the political century is over, and that all that's left is to shuffle cards on the cruise ship. The great disease of the 20th century was the politicization of life. The totalitarians, left and right, showed the way, politicizing everything: economics, education, art, religion, family life. Not even genetics could escape politics. One remembers with disbelief not just Hitler's eugenic lunacies but also Stalin's designation of Lysenko's crackpot genetics as official truth, enforced by secret police.

After such a century, it is a form of salvation, of social health, for politics to be in acute and precipitous decline. As a Portuguese ex-leftist said of his country's recent renaissance, "Portugal's success is that its politics no longer dominate everything."

No Need for Politics

This is less another "era of good feelings" than an era of no feelings. Americans have decided that politics has such slight purchase on problems, national (such as the deficit) or local (such as crime), that it merits no emotional investment from them.

George F. Will, *Newsweek*, September 9, 1991.

At its headiest, the aim of 20th century politics was the transformation of man and society by means of power. This great project—politics as redemption—has ended in failure on a breathtaking scale: not just economic and political but also ecological, spiritual and, not surprising for an enterprise of such overweening hubris, moral. The deeper meaning of the overthrow of communism is the realization that man can shape neither history nor society by Five-Year Plans, and that attempts to contradict this truth must end in the grotesque. The revulsion with politics reflects the view that when politicians go about tinkering with something as organic as a poor family or a rural community by means of a federal welfare program or an enormous dam, the law of unintended consequences prevails.

George Bush's great good fortune is that he is a man utterly incapable of vision at a time when the people do not want vision and do not need it. Vision is for Khomeini and Castro, for Jesse Jackson and Pat Robertson. Happily, if only for now, Americans will have none of it.

Which is why when almost every pundit wrings his hands in despair at low voter turnout—some even feel obliged to propose

creative schemes to induce people to vote—I am left totally un-
moved. Low voter turnout means that people see politics as
quite marginal to their lives, as neither salvation nor ruin. That
is healthy. Low voter turnout is a leading indicator of contentment. For a country founded on the notion that that government
is best that governs least, it seems entirely proper that Americans should in large numbers register a preference against politics by staying home on Election Day.

A few weeks ago, a producer from public television came to
ask my advice about planning coverage for the 1992 elections.
Toward the end, she raised a special problem: how to get young
adults interested in political coverage. I offered the opinion that
19-year-olds who sit in front of a television watching politics
could use professional help. At that age they should be playing
ball and looking for a date. They'll have time enough at my age
to worry about the mortgage and choosing a candidate on the
basis of his views on monetary policy.

To say that, of course, is to violate current League of Women
Voters standards of good citizenship. Let others struggle
valiantly to raise the political awareness of all citizens. Let them
rage against the tides of indifference. They will fail, and when
they do, relax. Remember that indifference to politics leaves all
the more room for the things that really count: science, art, religion, family and play.

Distinguishing Between Fact and Opinion

This activity is designed to help develop the basic reading and thinking skill of distinguishing between fact and opinion. Consider the following statement: "Voter participation in the United States has declined in the last fifty years." This is a factual statement because it could be checked by looking up voter turnout statistics for the pasty fifty years in a source such as an almanac. But the statement "People who do not vote are lazy and irresponsible" is an opinion. Some people refuse to vote because they do not agree with any of the candidates' positions or because they do not feel that their vote counts.

When investigating controversial issues, it is important that one be able to distinguish between statements of fact and statements of opinion. It is also important to recognize that not all statements of fact are true. They may appear to be true, but some are based on inaccurate or false information. For this activity, however, we are concerned with understanding the difference between those statements that appear to be factual and those that appear to be based primarily on opinion.

Most of the following statements are taken from the viewpoints in this chapter. Consider each statement carefully. *Mark O for any statement you believe is an opinion or interpretation of facts. Mark F for any statement you believe is a fact. Mark I for any statement you believe is impossible to judge.*

If you are doing this activity as a member of a class or group, compare your answers with those of other class or group members. Be able to defend your answers. You may discover that others come to different conclusions than you do. Listening to the reasons others present for their answers may give you valuable insights into distinguishing between fact and opinion.

> O = *opinion*
> F = *fact*
> I = *impossible to judge*

1. The United States, if one counts both its Presidential elections and its mid-term elections, now has the lowest rate of voter participation of any democracy in the world.
2. Since 1974, campaign spending for the United States House of Representatives has jumped from $53.5 million to $256.5 million.
3. Americans avoid voting because they are bored by politics, alienated, mistrustful of politicians, and/or suspicious of the political system.
4. In 1982, in California, there was a close race between former governor Edmund G. Brown Jr. and Senator Pete Wilson for Wilson's senate seat.
5. There is no question that the spiralling cost of campaigns is directly attributable to the widespread belief that demagogic advertising works.
6. People who vote are also likely to be people who patronize bake sales.
7. The Supreme Court ruled in *Buckley v. Valeo* that organizations independent of candidate and party had a right to participate in the political dialogue.
8. Alexis de Tocqueville said about American politics: "As the election draws near, the activity of intrigue and the agitation of the populace increase."
9. Washington, D.C., is a city in decline.
10. Nineteen-year-olds who sit in front of a television watching politics could use professional help. At that age they should be playing ball and looking for a date.
11. U.S. democracy is undergoing a slow and protracted death.
12. The book *The American Voter* found voter turnout to be markedly affected by the sense of citizen duty.
13. Populism's growth has been impressive, and its potential to revitalize the American political system is genuine.
14. Recent changes in national party rules, court decisions, and governmental policies have conspired to weaken local parties and political parties in general.
15. In 1960, E.E. Schattschneider described the limited American electorate as a "broadly based oligarchy."
16. The limited American electorate is a broadly based oligarchy.
17. The decomposition of parties and the decline in electoral turnout continue.
18. Since the 1960s, the United States has substantially liberalized its laws governing voter registration.
19. In 1988, more than 57.9 percent of every campaign dollar was allocated to television advertising.

Periodical Bibliography

The following articles have been selected to supplement the diverse views presented in this chapter.

James R. Boylan	"Where Have All the People Gone?" *Columbia Journalism Review*, May/June 1991.
Harry C. Boyte	"The Growth of Citizen Politics," *The Kettering Review*, Fall 1991. Available from the Kettering Foundation, 200 Commons Rd., Dayton, OH 45459-2799.
Mona Charen	"Failing to Vote Isn't So Bad," *Conservative Chronicle*, May 23, 1990. Available from PO Box 11297, Des Moines, IA 50340-1297.
Richard C. Harwood	"Citizens and Politics: A View from Main Street America," *The Kettering Review*, June 1991.
Douglas Jeffe and Sherry Bebitch Jeffe	"Absence Counts: Voting by Mail," *The American Enterprise*, November/December 1990.
Tom Kiely	"A Choice, Not an Echo?" *Technology Review*, August/September 1991.
James J. Kilpatrick	"No Need for National Voter Registration," *Human Events*, August 31, 1991. Available from 422 First St. SE, Washington, DC 20003.
James J. Kilpatrick	"Voter Registration Bill Is Tough to Swallow," *Conservative Chronicle*, June 26, 1991.
Erwin Knoll	"Making My Vote Count by Refusing to Cast It," *Peace & Democracy News*, Summer 1991.
Tibor R. Machan	"When Voting Makes No Sense," *The Freeman*, October 1988. Available from the Foundation for Economic Education, Inc., Irvington-on-Hudson, NY 10533.
The Nation	"Exchange," January 7-14, 1991.
Ed Rubenstein	"The Vanishing Voter," *National Review*, November 19, 1990.
Micah L. Sifry	"Let 'em Vote for 'None of the Above,'" *The Nation*, September 10, 1990.
Society	"Democratic Disparities," special section, July/August 1991.
U.S. Catholic	"Political Responsibility: Revitalizing American Democracy," *Origins*, October 24, 1991. Available from Catholic News Service, 3211 4th St. NE, Washington, DC 20017-1100.
George F. Will	"Voter Registration Bill Increases Fraud," *Conservative Chronicle*, September 18, 1991.

What Political Ideologies Are Important in the United States?

Chapter Preface

An ideology is any set of philosophical beliefs, often used to unite a group of people. American political ideologies encompass economic, foreign policy, and other issues that affect citizens. For example, the libertarian ideology includes the premise that government should not be involved in the lives and activities of citizens. Because of this ideology, libertarians value an expansion of freedom for both individuals and businesses. Libertarians take steps to reduce government regulation of business and to decrease government involvement in Americans' personal decisions. Consequently, they promote decriminalizing all "victimless" crimes such as drug use and prostitution, and they oppose all taxes.

Libertarians are only one example of the many influential ideologies in American life. Some of the others are conservatism, liberalism, and socialism. Traditionally, these ideologies have helped individuals and political parties set goals and determine steps to take to achieve these goals.

Many political analysts today question whether political ideologies have any meaning or serve any purpose for most Americans. In his book *Why Americans Hate Politics*, E.J. Dionne Jr. argues that the conservative and liberal ideologies that have dominated American politics since the 1960s are too extreme and do not represent the majority of Americans. For example, ideologies focus on such abstract concepts as the appropriate role of government and the extent to which the free market should dominate Americans' lives. But many Americans are not interested in these theories; they want to elect politicians with practical solutions to the nation's overwhelming problems. They want crime reduced, taxes lowered, and the homeless off the streets. Dionne believes the emphasis of politicians and political parties on ideology rather than practical solutions has made Americans apathetic toward politics.

Several authors in the following chapter, however, firmly stand behind their political ideologies and argue that Dionne and other critics do not understand the importance ideology plays in American politics. Any ideology, whether it be conservatism, populism, liberalism, or socialism, contributes to American political debate, they contend. Without ideologies, Americans and their political parties would be directionless, with no foundation upon which to base their goals and actions. The authors in this chapter debate this and other points concerning American political discourse.

"Conservatives have helped change the world for the better."

Conservatism Is a Vital Political Ideology

Edwin J. Feulner Jr.

Edwin J. Feulner Jr. is president of The Heritage Foundation, a well-known conservative think tank in Washington, D.C. In the following viewpoint, Feulner espouses his belief in conservatism as a political ideology. Conservatism enabled the United States to conquer Soviet communism, to promote democracy throughout the world, and to strengthen America's economy, the author maintains. Feulner asserts that conservatism has benefited America in the past, and can bring prosperity to the nation in the future.

As you read, consider the following questions:

1. What specific actions by the U.S. caused the collapse of Soviet communism, in Feulner's opinion?
2. What does the author believe conservatives must do to further their cause?
3. What evidence does Feulner give to prove that conservatism is gaining in popularity and power?

Excerpted from "Conservatism in a New Age" by Edwin J. Feulner Jr., *St. Croix Review*, June 1990. Reprinted with permission.

Let the record show that 1989 was the most significant year in the most important decade since World War II. But before the revisionists rewrite history and credit the global triumph of freedom to Carter-Mondale-Weicker-McGovernism, or to Soviet President Mikhail Gorbachev, let the record also show that the victory belongs to American conservatives.

Sure, liberals as well as conservatives "believe" in freedom and democracy. And they have every bit as much reason to celebrate the events in Eastern Europe as do Ronald Reagan, George Bush, Barry Goldwater, Ed Meese, and Ed Feulner.

But it wasn't the weak policies of the Seventies—the public retreat from world leadership, the humiliating self-doubt, the lonely walks in the Rose Garden, the "incurable" stagflation, the block-long gas lines, the malaise of the Misery Index—that prompted the Soviets to loosen their grip. Nor did they come around as a result of lectures on income redistribution by John Kenneth Galbraith or friendship visits by Armand Hammer.

U.S. Actions Force Soviet Response

Mikhail Gorbachev saw the handwriting on the wall. And what he saw was this: eight years (and still counting) of sustained U.S. economic expansion; determined U.S. efforts to rebuild its military arsenal after years of neglect; U.S.-built Stinger anti-aircraft missiles being effectively used by the Afghan freedom-fighters to shoot down Soviet aircraft; the Strategic Defense Initiative; NATO's strategic modernization program; unrelenting U.S. efforts through Voice of America, Radio Free Europe, and Radio Liberty to explain to people living behind the Iron Curtain not only what was happening in the West, but in their own countries as well; President Reagan's oft-criticized war of words; and last but not least, the embarrassing failure of state socialism, an economic system hailed as the wave of the future by many of America's leading leftist intellectuals. These are the realities, brought about by the conservative policies of the Reagan-Bush era, that cut gaping holes in the barbed wire of the Iron Curtain and turned the Berlin Wall into another capitalist triumph: historical souvenirs at Macy's and other fine stores. Indeed, the very policies that brought renewal to the West and forced Soviet rulers to confront reality are the ones that liberals have fought and belittled every step of the way. Those of us on the receiving end of their endless barbs have every reason to gloat.

But even these developments are already history. Perhaps the ultimate tribute to conservative ideas and policies is what lies ahead. Because it is to us—to the free-market ideas of F.A. Hayek, Adam Smith, and Milton Friedman and to people like Richard Rahn of the U.S. Chamber of Commerce, William

Dennis of the National Federation of Independent Business, and Stuart Butler of The Heritage Foundation—that the governments of Eastern Europe are now turning for advice. They have seen the future and it's not the vaunted Soviet model, which has brought them nothing but poverty. Only on U.S. college campuses does the socialist dream linger on. In Warsaw, Tallinn, Prague, and Budapest, they don't want lectures on income redistribution and capitalist exploitation; they want income and capitalism. . . .

Conservative Victory

America's conservatives have won a great victory, after seven decades of struggle. From President Wilson's dispatch of troops to the Russian arctic to President Reagan's expedition to Moscow for conferring with Gorbachev, the great American Republic wrestled with the Russian bear; and the Western concept of ordered freedom contended against the ideology of Marxism. Alexis de Tocqueville foresaw that tremendous contest, which now has been decided in favor of the United States of America and in favor of the politics of prudence and prescription.

Russell Kirk, *The Heritage Lectures*, June 14, 1990.

All of this was a great triumph for American conservatism. President Reagan not only strengthened U.S. defenses, but he made clear that the United States was through winking at Soviet adventurism. While the Soviet economy was disintegrating (as it continues to do), the U.S. economy boomed. Even Reagan's deregulation of oil prices helped turn the tide against the Soviets, triggering a worldwide price drop that cut sharply into the Soviets' hard currency earning from oil exports.

This is how we helped make a new world. The Kremlin's leaders didn't suddenly mutate into Jeffersonian democrats. They were pushed there by the same changed "correlation of forces" that caused Soviet General Secretary Leonid Brezhnev to gloat a decade earlier about the "seriously weakened" state of world capitalism.

More than anything else, all of these momentous changes mean one thing for conservatives: we have to recognize that the world is dramatically different than the one we inherited from the Carter-era doomsayers a decade ago. And we have to act accordingly. This does not mean compromising in any way the principles in which conservatives believe—limited government, individual liberty, free enterprise, and peace through strength.

But we have to recognize that we have a chance like none other since the New Deal to reshape the political landscape, and take advantage of it. The future is still up for grabs. In the '80s conservatives successfully popularized conservative principles as principles. In the '90s our goal must be to translate these *principles* into policy, and in that respect the fight has just begun. . . .

Empowering the People

The conservative agenda can never be brought to full flower simply by rearranging the deck chairs on the Titanic called the federal bureaucracy. For the conservative revolution to take root firmly, we must empower Americans to run their own lives. This means, for example, giving parents the freedom to choose the schools their children attend, empowering tenants to manage the public-housing projects where they live, and providing businesses incentives to invest in poor inner-city neighborhoods. As President Bush has said, the best anti-poverty program is a job—a real job in the private sector, with a real future.

"By supporting empowerment," Heritage Director of Domestic Policy Studies Stuart Butler wrote in *National Review*, "conservative poverty-warriors can trigger confrontations between the poor and the welfare state that serves them so badly. These confrontations will help conservatives to build the coalitions needed to tip the political balance in favor of their proposals."

It's not enough anymore simply to discredit liberalism; in the new age, conservatives must show we can succeed where liberalism has failed. That failure is everywhere. Yet in such areas as environmental policy, health care, and day-care, liberal members of Congress are promoting more of the same: policies that, by the end of the '90s could make the deficits of the '80s seem piddling.

The good news is that conservatism appears fully up to the task. The left, though unsure of what to make of Eastern Europe's passion for free minds and free markets, is right about one thing: the collapse of the Soviet Empire means conservatives don't have to spend as much time worrying about the threat of communist aggression. But instead of spreading despair among conservative troops, this should help liberate us, and free us to tackle many of those other problems that despite their importance and even urgency have seemed less important, less urgent when compared to the task of national survival.

Intellectually, conservatism has never been healthier. Four of our own—Milton Friedman, F. A. Hayek, George Stigler, and James Buchanan—have been recognized in recent years with Nobel Prizes in economics, at one time the exclusive preserve of the left. In other fields as well, conservative academics and intellectuals have helped reshape the way America thinks. In the 1970s, for example, who had heard of Charles Murray, Stuart Butler, George Gilder, Daniel Pipes, Kim Holmes, or Richard

McKenzie? You can bet they will all be heard from time and time again in the decade ahead.

While conservatives have sometimes fumbled the political ball in Washington, we now are better prepared than ever to help shape policy at the local and state level. Effective conservative research and advocacy organizations now exist in more than half the states, from Washington, California, and Arizona in the West to Pennsylvania, Massachusetts, and Connecticut in the East, and more will appear as their successes grow. Already some of these organizations have left their marks, offering alternative solutions to such problems as educational decline, prison overcrowding, and public transit financing.

Conservatism Is Rooted in Human Nature

Conservatism is at least as instinctive as it is intellectual. When it triumphs it is a victory of the visceral over the vaporous, drawing on values and loyalties deeply imbedded in human nature and the American character.

Aram Bakshian Jr., *National Review*, June 24, 1991.

There is now a conservative public-interest law movement, where a decade ago there was nothing. Conservative journals, modeled after the *Dartmouth Review*, established several years ago by Heritage alumnae Benjamin Hart and Dinesh D'Souza and several of their classmates, now flourish on dozens of college campuses, from Harvard to Stanford and Berkeley. And even the publishing industry—including Macmillan's Free Press, Rutgers University's Transaction Books, Universe Books, Madison Books, University Press of America, Stein and Day, and Basil Blackwell—has discovered, as the traditional conservative publishers Lexington Books, Green Hill, and Regnery Gateway learned years ago, that Americans who buy books want both sides of the story. In other words, conservative books sell.

Conservatives have spent the last forty-five years preventing the left from dismantling the barricades against Soviet communism. Today all the world can appreciate the wisdom of our struggle, derided for so many years, and in so many ways, by those who opposed us.

Now conservatives are ready to do battle on other fronts. Stuart Butler, Jack Kemp, and Anna Kondratas propose a conservative war on poverty. Warren Brookes sees the environment as the great battleground of the 1990s. The fight against drugs demands our attention—as does the war against public schools that are a public disgrace.

The world, too, is still a dangerous place. The Soviets, who possess enough nuclear fire-power to incinerate most of the globe, face troubled times; and instability in the Soviet Union poses great challenges and grave threats to the West. Iraq is building long-distance missiles, and may again be developing nuclear arms. Much of Latin America is still in turmoil. And Africa: the legacy of socialism can be seen everywhere as the malnourished and starving and near-corpses compete for less and less bounty.

By not deviating from bedrock principles, conservatives have helped change the world for the better. But there are many battles still to fight. Nineteen-eighty-nine was a remarkable year in the annals of freedom. We intend to see that the 1990s are remembered as the decade of freedom—and of unprecedented opportunity for each and every American.

"The conservative cause has become a spent volcano, still spitting and sputtering, but no longer capable of reshaping the political landscape."

Conservatism Is a Declining Political Ideology

David N. Dinkins

Conservatism is a dying ideology that has lost the power to affect social policy in the United States, David N. Dinkins contends in the following viewpoint. Dinkins acknowledges that conservatism wielded significant political power in the 1980s, but asserts that now the ideology is hopelessly outdated and no longer represents most Americans. Dinkins, a Democrat, was elected mayor of New York City in 1989.

As you read, consider the following questions:

1. What role does race play in the downfall of conservatism, according to Dinkins?
2. How did the conservatism of the 1980s affect America, in the author's opinion?
3. Why does Dinkins believe the conservatives failed?

The crest of the conservative flood has passed. The Republicans still occupy the White House, but the conservative coalition has lost its way. It no longer can dominate public and social policy. It has lost its ability to intimidate so many into silence and despair. A decade of reaction and retrenchment has begun to yield to a resurgence of progressive ideals.

The approach is not novel. The same process marked the 1920s in America, a time when cities and states were forced to design solutions of their own because of the withdrawal of the Federal government from the national stage. Many of them became the basis for Federal action in the 1930s.

As was true in the 1930s, we have a lot to overcome today. In the 1980s, we saw the ethics and dreams of Martin Luther King, Jr., and John F. Kennedy traded in for selfishness and callousness. The national government once again withdrew from American cities, but the national problems did not fade away.

We watched as the Federal government washed away our national priorities with a wave of tax cuts that provided quick stimulation in exchange for a crushing burden of debt. It was cruelty masquerading as patriotism.

Each of the pillars upon which the conservative coalition was built—the Cold War, the politics of division and exclusion at home, the attack on a woman's right to make her own choices about reproduction, and regressive economics—has cracked and in some cases crumbled. For decades, the fear of communism abroad blocked the path to progress here at home. Ideas were tested not for their strength and effectiveness, but for the degree of their orientation to the right or left.

The progressive income tax, Social Security, labor laws, civil rights, national health insurance, gun control—all were suspect, all were sinister and socialistic, and all were fought bitterly by the right. The spectre of communism also dominated domestic politics, distorting our budgets and disrupting our pursuit of social and political fairness.

Military might became the sole measure of national security, leaving no room in our calculation of American strength for infant mortality, literacy, or economic opportunity.

During the 1980s, the Pentagon budget doubled while Federal housing assistance was cut more than 75%. Today, the conservatives cling to a war-time budget while the rest of the world celebrates the end of the Cold War.

No Enemy, No Energy

In January, 1990, I joined my fellow mayors in Washington to call for a redirection of Federal spending from the Defense Department to American cities. Peace can bring us a tangible dividend, and we need that peace dividend to make our country stronger so that we can continue to assist those in Eastern Europe and elsewhere who will call on us again to lend a hand. The revolutions in Eastern Europe and the Soviet Union have created a dilemma for the conservatives. Without communism they have no enemy, and without an enemy they have no energy. Saddam Hussein is no substitute for the Russian bear.

One Administration official has declared that the end of the Cold War is the "end of history," and he may be correct, at least for the extreme right. There still must come a revolution in South Africa, and the students of Tiananmen Square must yet see their vision realized, but the Iron Curtain has been lifted.

Lacking Ideas

Let me propose a heretical idea—the liberals are not out of ideas, that it is the conservatives, today, who are stale. . . . Conservatives were successful because they worked extremely hard to master ideas and then to translate them into a winning philosophical and political vision. Conservatives won the '80s because they earned it.

But we don't deserve it any more. Our major publications repeat the solutions of the past, and we cling to "leaders" without any ideas and with few convictions.

Donald Devine, *The Washington Times*, September 30, 1991.

To the conservatives, the end of the Cold War is just the first of many woes. There also is the end of the politics of racial antagonism. Since Richard Nixon, the Republicans' electoral dominance has been based on a southern strategy. The conservative crusade began in 1980 not by ringing the liberty bell in Philadelphia, Pa., but by winking at the enemies of liberty in Philadelphia, Miss.

Throughout the 1980s, those on the right resisted every effort to swing open the doors of opportunity more widely. They opposed the Equal Rights Amendment and equal pay for equal work. They struggled against the Voting Rights Act.

Their insensitivity to prejudice has been indefensible, but their attitude grows from ignorance and isolation. The Republicans sought not diversity, but uniformity. Of the more than 400 Federal judicial appointments made during the 1980s, only 26 were racial minorities and just 32 were women. The Bush Administration still has only one African-American, one Hispanic, and two women in the Cabinet.

When I declared my candidacy for Mayor of New York City, most thought that it would take a miracle for me to defeat first a popular three-term mayor, Ed Koch, and then a powerful prosecutor, Rudolph Giuliani. Nevertheless, African-Americans, Latinos, and Asians; Catholics and Jews; gays and lesbians; persons with disabilities and those who are able-bodied all came together in celebration of diversity. They voted their hopes, not their fears.

When the people of Virginia joined in, they threw the southern strategy and its politics of exclusion onto the ash heap of history. They redefined the realm of the possible for millions of Americans who now can dream again of holding public office.

Abortion Rights

The right won't be running against abortion, either. In November, 1989, voters in New York, New Jersey, and Virginia sent strong signals to those who would let government interfere with a woman's right to choose. Who would have thought a year ago that even the chairman of the Republican National Committee, Lee Atwater, would claim to be agnostic on abortion? The effort to make God a partisan political being has failed.

Finally, there was Reaganomics. More than anything else, the Reagan Revolution was predicated on the proposition that the government should lavish its largesse upon those with the most. No tax cut was too irresponsible, no special benefit too unfair, and no deregulation too extreme.

What a dowry it left us. The latest bill for the S&L bail-out is $300,000,000,000 and growing. The interest on just that portion of the debt, the amount needed to bail out the savings and loans, would go a long way toward rebuilding our urban housing stock to eliminate homelessness.

The Republican economic miracle turned out to be a mirage—all of it except for the national debt. That has proved to be painfully real, all three trillion dollars of it.

The conservative cause has become a spent volcano, still spitting and sputtering, but no longer capable of reshaping the political landscape. Sadly for Americans, though, the land the conservatives have left behind is scorched and scarred. The challenges they ignored—crack and crime, AIDS and education, homelessness and hunger, poverty and pollution—remain very much with us.

The conservatives regaled us with tales of resurgence while the rest of the world went whizzing by. So now we can remember the touching speeches and sentimental images of the 1980s while we travel across roads and bridges that are crumbling, to take our kids to schools that aren't teaching, to prepare them for life in a global economy that suddenly threatens to leave them behind.

Where are the solutions? Many of us outside of Washington are hard at work defining our goals, refining our methods, and preparing solutions for the 1990s. From the ground up, we're

125

building a new foundation upon the rubble of the conservative decade. If progressive ideas were a stock, now would be the time to buy.

We must start with a fundamental commitment to democracy—a passion for participation that is opening our government to those who previously have not been invited or allowed in. It has to belong to no elite or narrow interest. We need an open forum that hears diverse views and voices before it decides, a democracy that appeals to what is best in us and strives to bring us together. This is not merely a matter of principle—it's practical politics.

A Lost Cause

American conservatism is a failure, and all the think tanks, magazines, direct mail barons, inaugural balls, and campaign buttons cannot disguise or alter that. Virtually every cause to which conservatives have attached themselves for the past three generations has been lost, and the tide of political and cultural battle is not likely to turn anytime soon.

Samuel Francis, *Chronicles*, May 1991.

Our society is a gorgeous mosaic of race and religious faith, of national origin and sexual orientation. No one person and no one group possibly can understand the ways and the worries of all. A government that includes all in the process will exclude fewer in the result. Representation—real representation—will reduce the alienation and frustration that too often characterize our society. Broad-based government is better government. That's the approach that will be required for this nation to realize its true potential.

Above all else, the problems and perils of American society today are matters of public safety. Crime and drugs—and the fear and failures they cause—are tearing away at the fabric of our society.

Our cities are under siege. Entire neighborhoods across this nation have become free-fire zones. Children come to school wearing beepers that link them not to their teachers or their parents, but to the drug suppliers who command their highest loyalties. Some of our housing projects literally have become base camps for armies of drug dealers. High atop the gleaming skyscrapers that exemplify our economic predominance, young and not-so-young professionals—well-educated men and women with substantial monetary resources—foolishly remain drawn to the allure of cocaine and other illicit drugs.

We must take back our streets, by night as well as by day. We have to return law and order by making the police part of our communities and asking our communities to participate in policing.

However, respect for the law—and for each other—requires more than better policing; more than tougher statutes against group violence and bias crimes; more than a ban on assault weapons; more even than creating a penalty of life in prison without parole for those who commit the worst crimes—literally, to lock them up and throw away the key.

Assuming Responsibility

What matters most is not our programs, as important as they are, but our values, especially individual responsibility. For too long, we have been hesitant to require from all who share this society that they carry their portion of the load. We must not allow barriers and obstacles to become an excuse. Life is not always fair and it's hard to get ahead, but each of us has an obligation to work hard, respect the law, be disciplined and strong, and take responsibility for our actions. . . .

At the same time, we must recognize that we're all born into a world we did not make; that responsibility comes more easily with resources; and that individual effort must be tied to an ethic of social obligation. . . .

More than anything else, the failure of governments on all levels in recent years has been their inability to conform public policy to public values. The result of the Reagan Revolution must not become an even deeper distrust and disillusion in the purpose of politics and the power of government. The conservatives failed not because they tried to remake the world, but because their vision and their values were so dangerously divorced from the reality of the society they temporarily dominated.

As we shed the weight of the past and seek a new consensus for the 1990s, let us recognize that new times require new approaches and new solutions. . . .

Let us always remember that the politics of this nation must reflect the people of this nation—a diverse populace that demands democracy and participation; believes in individual responsibility *and* social obligation; works hard and wants government to work equally hard to meet *its* fiscal responsibilities; always comes forward when called on to contribute; and is prepared to move ahead. This nation is ready for its own democracy movement, an era when tolerance and mutual respect will mean greater freedom for each of us.

"A strong, assertive liberalism is a prerequisite for the changes that are needed in America."

Liberalism Would Strengthen America

Dissent

The following viewpoint, a statement prepared and issued by 159 supporters of liberalism, appeared in *Dissent* magazine, a quarterly socialist journal. In it, the authors argue that the United States has suffered economically and socially from the conservatism of the Reagan and Bush administrations. Poverty has increased and civil rights have been harmed, the authors contend. Because liberal values include helping the oppressed and working for equality, the authors believe that a renewal of liberalism can bring prosperity and increased social justice to America.

As you read, consider the following questions:

1. What is the cause of much of America's social misery, in the opinion of the authors?
2. Why do the authors believe the free market should be regulated?
3. Describe the kind of society the authors envision for America.

Excerpted, with permission, from "A Statement for the Democratic Left" by *Dissent* magazine, Fall 1991, © 1991 by the Foundation for the Study of Independent Social Ideas, Inc.

The collapse of communism and the 1991 military victory in the Gulf were greeted with smugness. One might suppose that America's triumph means that our troubles are over—that all we need from the future is more of the past.

But beneath the surface, there is profound uneasiness, a sense of things gone wrong, an atmosphere of alarm and anxiety. Everyone can point to signs of social decline, even social breakdown—poverty, crime, drugs, the breakdown of cities, the savings and loan crisis, the failure to provide decent health insurance for millions of people. The social contract—never adequate, but a major step forward—created by American liberalism, through the New Deal and its successors, said that the federal government has a responsibility to guarantee the accountability of the institutions on which the country depends. Reaganism, a partial counterrevolution, could not quite destroy this social contract, but it severely weakened it, both in terms of legislation and popular thought. Reaganism and its puny offspring in the Bush administration are a major source of the social squalor increasingly afflicting this country.

The United States and much of the rest of the industrial world are burning up the future through careless energy policies. American political culture seems most invigorated only at moments when it can confront an external enemy. Meanwhile, social misery has become normal; indignation is diverted and blocked; protest is scattered and incoherent.

Much of today's social misery is avoidable—it is due, in good part, to economic and political arrangements rigged against, or at best indifferent to, the common good. Beneath the many varieties of social misery is a pattern: the systematic maldistribution of resources and of government expenditures.

The Neglect of Social Ills

Has there ever before been an administration in Washington so openly indifferent to the condition of the country? Even the Reaganites had policies to offer—bad ones, but at least policies. But the Bush administration, from moral cynicism or social ignorance or both, behaves as if all the social ills that are visible in the streets simply do not exist or can be cured through the mysterious ministrations of the market. Neglect is the policy of Bush, indifference the motivating outlook.

A great question must now be posed, and if there were a sufficiently vigorous opposition in Congress and public life, it would be hammering away at this question: If the United States could succeed in transporting half a million soldiers and a vast quantity of war materiel within a few months to engage in the Gulf War, why does our government seem so feeble, so lax (and relaxed) before the task of mobilizing American resources to cope with our growing poverty, the shame of homelessness, the collapse of the cities, the breakdown of the infrastructure, the failures of education, the scandals of racism and sexism? It is sometimes said that these tasks are more difficult than conducting a war thousands of miles from our shores. If so, then let us, through renewed common action, call upon greater social, moral, and financial resources. To see the social ills of America as "natural" or beyond remedy by human beings is to acquiesce in the ideology of reaction.

Issues to Address

Here, in briefest summary, are a few of the issues—neglected, denied—that our country must confront:

• The government defines poverty at an extremely low level. Even so, some thirty-two million Americans, or 15 percent of the population, according to official statistics, are poor. . . .

• American society has acquired a shape that, from a democratic perspective, is unjust. The median net worth of the top 1 percent of households is twenty-two times greater than the median net worth of the other 99 percent! If we consider "net financial assets"—a household's net worth minus equity in homes and vehicles—the gap is even wider: the median of the top 1 percent of households in the United States is 237 times greater than the median of the other 99 percent. That is not what a democratic society should look like. . . .

The Principles of Liberalism

The principles of liberalism . . . are older than all existing constitutions and are more deeply rooted than any formulation of them that can be put into words. . . .

The liberal philosophy holds that enduring governments must be accountable to someone beside themselves; that a government responsible only to its own conscience is not for long tolerable. It holds that since any government is liable to fail, there is needed a method of changing the governors without wrecking the state. It holds that unless there is a method, be it through elections or otherwise, by which the governed can make their views effective in some proportion to their weight, the nation is at the mercy of violence in the form of terrorism, assassination, conspiracy, mass compulsion, and civil war.

Walter Lippmann, *Vanity Fair*, November 1934.

• One of the few triumphs in the last two decades has been the rise of the feminist movement. But the gains have been only partial, and some have been lost again. Economic inequality persists, and so do political and social inequality. . . .

- Victims of violence are to be found disproportionately among racial minorities, the elderly, homosexuals, children, and women beaten by husbands and partners—wherever people are vulnerable. The homicide rate among young men in the United States is far higher—four to seventy-three times—than in other industrial countries. Yet somehow we have become accustomed to seeing this condition as "natural.". . .

Blacks and Poverty

- A generation has passed since the civil rights revolution, which remains a great victory of radical democratic action in America. Yet for too many people race is still destiny. The black middle class has prospered to some degree, but the ghetto decays. Men in Harlem live shorter lives than men in Bangladesh. Black family income in 1987 was only 56 percent of whites'. The median net worth of whites is 11.7 times that of blacks. Two-thirds of black households have zero or negative net financial assets—compared with 30 percent of white households. Race forms an economic tier: whites on top, blacks on the bottom.

While attitudes in some parts of American society become more reactionary and bigoted with regard to race and ethnic differences, the actual racial and ethnic composition of the population is becoming ever more varied. America needs more of a liberal sensibility on these matters, not less. We need to reassert the democratic goal of racial integration.

- During the Reagan years, the United States spent $2.4 trillion dollars financing an overblown military machine. The end of the cold war created an opportunity to apply some of the country's wealth to social reconstruction (and to ease the burdens of transformation in Eastern Europe and the Third World). Yet Congress has only nibbled away at the Pentagon budget. . . .

There is no single cause of, no single solution to, the dangers and problems we face today. We believe, however, that the question of the management and ownership of the economy is fundamental. The current fad for "free" or unregulated market—a figment of pure ideology—cannot lead to equitable socioeconomic solutions. Markets constitute a system for distributing goods and capital, and it is all but meaningless to speak of or evaluate markets apart from the social system and economic structure within which they function To abolish markets altogether would be foolish, but to let them operate without substantial regulation must surely lead to greater concentration of wealth in fewer hands. By itself the market cannot generate social equality or justice. It cannot generate a feeling of community. It cannot look out for the environment, for the rights of the oppressed, or even, at times, for the long-range interest of its own most enthusiastic champions.

131

Only social action through government intervention and through the efforts of trade unions and other large groups of mobilized citizens can do these things. But who will propose and initiate democratic social action for substantial reform in a day when the "free market" has become a popular ideology? . . . A strong, assertive liberalism is a prerequisite for the changes that are needed in America, as well as for the renewal of a linked or adjacent democratic left.

This country needs a democratic left—a movement that will speak about the democratization of society, that will seek to control business and to stimulate investment and innovation for the general good, that will create a basis for majority electoral coalitions. The social basis for such a left already exists—in the unions and in women's movements, in movements for ecology, for the rights of minorities and immigrants. A desire for such a movement isn't hard to detect, either—among educated young people, for instance, who wish to pursue careers devoted to social progress, egalitarianism, the sharing of privileges.

The Government's Duty

The liberal party is a party which believes that, as new conditions and problems arise beyond the power of men and women to meet as individuals, it becomes the duty of the government itself to find new remedies with which to meet them.

Franklin D. Roosevelt, *The Public Papers and Addresses of Franklin D. Roosevelt,* 1938-1950.

For a renewed democratic left, intellectual work matters. Some of the worst notions of the 1980s—supply-side economics, the supposed failure of Great Society programs, the claimed superiority of right-wing over left-wing dictatorships, the presumed American lag in nuclear arms—emanated from intellectuals and well-placed publicists. Since the late 1960s, neoconservatives have not been bashful about promoting their policies—and perhaps even more important, striking an emotional tone, a sour vision. In an America where many felt threatened by crime, neoconservatives offered rationalizations for social recoil. . . .

The vistas of potential success for a reformed and consistently democratic left in America may at the moment seem small. But our history of political and social movements offers a different vista. In this country the great majority enjoy a significant degree of democratic freedom; we have, in spite of everything, made some progress in creating opportunities for groups previously discriminated against; we have, however inadequately, managed to introduce some Social Security, universal education,

Medicare, and other benefits. Such democratic successes are largely due to ever-recurring waves of radical reform.

The American Revolution itself, then the Jacksonian reforms of the 1820s, the abolitionist movement, and the war to free the slaves, the farm populists of the 1890s, the Socialists and Wobblies of the 1910s, the seventy-year-long movement for women's suffrage, the New Dealers and unionists of the thirties, the civil rights movement of the fifties and sixties, the antiwar mobilizers of the sixties and early seventies, the social criticism of writers like Michael Harrington, the feminist movement of the sixties into the present, the movements to extend individual freedom in new directions, the ecology movement of the present moment—these represent the great tradition of American reform. Every twenty or thirty years throughout the history of the United States, there has been a wave of such movements, representing the strength of American life.

Hope for a Better Society

We do not believe that human society is ever likely to know perfection. But neither are we willing to stare at every calamity and limply conclude that no solutions can be found. A better society is entirely imaginable in this country—a society that enjoys the freedoms that have always been celebrated by the liberal tradition and that moves toward the egalitarianism, the social justice, and liberation from alienated work that have always been the goals of socialism. It is possible to imagine a society in which working women and men through unions and other institutions will be able to shape the economy and their working lives, and will not have to surrender to corporate power; a society in which the poor will rise at least to the minimal levels of a decent life; a society that can arouse itself for moral and democratic aims and not cave in to the media campaigns and manipulations of powerful elites. We want a world in which the life-chances of children are no longer so dramatically predictable on the basis of economic condition, race, and gender as they are today. Something is wrong with a culture that dismisses such concerns as foolish or naive.

There is a democratic dream to be renewed. It is the practical dream of libertarians like Thomas Paine and feminists like Elizabeth Cady Stanton, of socialists and trade unionists like Eugene V. Debs and A. Philip Randolph, of civil rights champions like Rosa Parks and Martin Luther King, Jr., the dream of rebellious slaves, indignant trade unionists, human-rights workers, defenders of individual freedom and of the earth and the air. In the name of the common good that always requires uncommon work, let us do what we can to renew that dream.

133

"*Liberalism is no longer—if it ever was—the party of reason.*"

Liberalism Is a Harmful Political Ideology

Horatio Galba

Liberalism is a worthless ideology that has resulted in danger-ous U.S. foreign policy decisions and ineffective economic mea-sures, Horatio Galba argues in the following viewpoint. Liberalism encourages diplomacy that exposes the U.S. to its en-emies and promotes economic measures that redistribute wealth rather than create it, Galba maintains. For these reasons, the au-thor believes that liberalism has only harmed America. Galba is the European correspondent for *California Review*, a monthly newspaper of conservative opinion published by students at the University of California at San Diego.

As you read, consider the following questions:

1. What examples does the author give of liberal foreign policy decisions that have harmed the U.S.?
2. Why does Galba believe the liberal approach to foreign trade is inconsistent?
3. How have liberal values harmed American culture, in Galba's opinion?

Horatio Galba, "Liberalism and Rationality," *California Review*, October 1988. Reprinted with permission.

In the longstanding war between liberals and conservatives I hope that I am not the only one to have noticed that in recent years liberals have placed themselves not only *contra* conservatism, but also *contra* reason. Just as Norman Podhoretz believes that if George Orwell were alive today he'd be a neo-conservative, so am I convinced that if Aristotle were alive today he'd vote a straight Republican ticket. Here's why:

Foreign Policy. Though an internationalist in theory, the liberal's heart lies in social and economic reform at home—and indeed, when he turns his attention to foreign affairs, his foreign policy, when it is interventionist, tends toward an attempt to export American social programs abroad: Tennesse Valley Authority Projects for South Vietnam, desegregation for South Africa, welfare for Central America.

The defense budget is, for the liberal, a burden on the coffers of the federal government that would be better spent on the homeless, the poor, and other domestic groups worthy, to his mind, of support.

And though the liberal believes in international law and the existence of some sort of international morality on whose side we should be, defense spending worries him, because deep down the liberal distrusts the use of American power as much, if not more than, the aggressiveness of America's enemies. So while the liberal will pronounce himself opposed to Communist expansionism, he will at the same time believe that the use, size, and capabilities of American power must also be constrained lest we be tempted, by having power, into using it unwisely, provoking our enemies by standing up to them with more than mere words (though even words can heighten tensions), and diverting money from necessary domestic programs supporting day care for the children of working mothers. Thus the foreign policy of the liberal runs the risk of servility to interest groups at home and powerful enemies abroad.

The Importance of Foreign Affairs

It also sets traditional wisdom on its ear by setting "low politics" above "high politics"—baldly, economics above diplomacy. It is an obvious lesson of history that it is in the conduct of international affairs that countries either ensure their survival or perish. It has always been and will always be the main purpose of government to secure the nation from its enemies foreign and domestic. It is difficult, if not impossible, to believe that the liberal is capable of dealing with foreign enemies or of recognizing domestic ones. For deep in the insular liberal heart is his not so secret fear that Ronald Reagan and "the radical right" were as much, if not greater a threat to peace than are the Soviets and their minions. For example, when the Sandinistas raided the

Contra camps in Honduras in March of 1988, Democratic Congressmen did not leap to rhetorically denounce the Sandinistas, but attacked the Reagan administration for engineering an excuse to send more troops to Honduras. And what can one say of an ideology that believes in upholding arms limitation agreements with the Soviets even when the Soviets are violating them, and believes itself in violating treaty obligations to America's allies when it is inconvinient to act on them as the Democratic Congress did to South Vietnam in 1975?

LIFE, LIBERTY AND THE PURSUIT OF HAPPINESS!

Chuck Asay by permission of the *Colorado Springs Gazette-Telegraph*.

Historically, liberals have fought many wars, but nowadays they tend to limit themselves to wars on poverty (which they never seem to win and which reason and empirical data suggest they are attacking in the wrong way—so much the worse for reason and empirical data), wars on our allies (trade wars), and wars on drug exporting countries (except Castro's Cuba and the Communist bloc, because they are our enemies and we don't want to antagonize them).

An Unreasonable Ideology

It would strike the rationalist that a liberal policy is opposed to history, to tradition, and to reason. A country that thinks its enemies are just misunderstood friends; whose diplomacy is conducted openly in international forum where posture-striking is *de rigeur*; rather than among professional, cosmopolitan, realist, diplomatists; and whose intellectual interests are parochial and whose foreign policy consists of exporting that parochialism abroad and enforcing it on our allies while we try to pacify our enemies as we pacify the poor—with money and words of encouragement (they have a great deal to teach us); is a country that will help mightily in its own extinction. This is a policy rather at odds with reason.

Economic Policy. Socialists in France are doing it, Communists in China are doing it, and even Ronald Reagan did it. What they are all doing is promoting free market, *laissez-faire*, capitalism. And liberals? Well, money is the root of all evil, so we should give more of it to the poor and keep it out of the hands of the rich. Liberals like capitalism okay if it is well-regulated, state directed, and if profits don't go to producers but are given to the underclass to spend on cholesterol-induced diseases.

Liberals introduced the world to the free market and free trade, but they have turned their backs on their own legacy—presumably because it has succeeded in creating the wealthiest societies in history and a broad middle class that left-wing intellectuals sneer at. And because it succeeded, it left liberals with precious little to do except to reform it to death.

Having become economic interventionalists at home, they have turned towards protectionism abroad. Liberals, though softhearted to the Third World, are willing to hang tough against Third World countries that are actually improving themselves and doing well economically. Liberals are nationalists when it comes to protecting the people who elect them from economic competition.

Irrational Policies

But they show the same split personality—or incoherence—when it comes to foreign trade that they do when it comes to foreign policy. They were in favor of expanding trade and loans to Communist countries because they threaten us and we want them to like us, and they erected sanctions against South Africa because it doesn't threaten us, has been our ally in two world wars, and is reforming. And they pushed for further sanctions because the original sanctions put blacks out of work, put more business in the hands of Afrikaners, added fuel to an already tense situation, undercut the most liberal segment of South African society, led to the growth of the really radical right, diminished American influence in the country, and now, of course, because the government is trying to liberalize itself again with a Great Indaba. Does that make sense? Does the answer to the non-problem of Reagonomics that has cured the previously seemingly incurable dual-headed disease of inflation and unemployment lie in the *dirigiste* economics of John Kenneth Galbraith, Felix Rohatyn, and Lester Thurow who believe that bureaucrats are better investors than businessmen? And if the budget deficit is a problem, who is more likely to curse it: those oh-so-hard-hearted Republicans or those compassionate, caring, bleeding-heart liberals?

The liberal position on economics is staunchly irrational because it is not based on the logical end of economics—economic growth. It is based on redistribution, on pacifying interest groups, and, inevitably, on helping our foes and hurting our friends—one of liberalism's constant and most irrational goals.

Social Policy. The parochialism that short-circuits liberal foreign policy is what also destroys liberal social policy—which is largely a policy in support of irresponsibility. Just as the liberal believes that the United States will always be powerful no matter how weak it becomes in relation to its enemies, and that it will always be wealthy no matter how much we rob from the productive to give to the unproductive, so too does he believe that social and cultural conservatism is a given, something that one can always return to, but that is restrictive of human freedom. Liberals, therefore, tend to give a wink and a nod to movement of artistic, social, and personal "liberation." "If it feels good, do it," (though this has of necessity been amended recently to "If it feels good, do it, but use a condom and a sterilized needle, both which will be provided by taxpayers and be available in handy dispensers at college dormitory restrooms").

The Wrong Kind of Productivity

This is an especially touchy field for liberals because though free love and drug-induced euphoria have their attractions, many Americans have come to feel that American productivity should make it in fields other than teenage pregnancies, illegitimacy, abortion, and drug-related violence and death. Liberals pawned it to mercenaries in league with the Contras; and as for teenage pregnancies, illegitimacy, and abortion, the answer, of course, is more sex education—despite the fact that all these banes have risen as sex education has spread.

One wonders whether liberals have any idea what true education really is. Liberals believe in spending more money on education because parents, who vote, want their children well educated. But it does not cost a great deal of money to assign students books of enduring worth and hold them accountable for mastering them. It *does* cost a lot of money to turn schools into audio-visual amusement parks complete with Mustangs for driver's training, counsellors and emporia for sex education and contraception, and video equipment for courses in creative film-making.

In education, as in everything else, liberals are wedded to interest groups. They are in favor of select *interest groups in education* not *excellence in education*. Excellence is elitist and therefore anti-egalitarian and anti-democratic. It is elitist to study academic subjects at the expense of those subjects that are more practical to the average person—typing, home economics for boys (to break down stereotypes), and wood shop for girls. In the academic subjects themselves, history becomes ethnohistory, sex-based history, and class struggle history; English becomes popular culture as philosophy, science fiction as literature, and creative writing as therapy; soon, no doubt, mathematics will be turned into a science with no wrong answers.

Liberalism Destroyed American Culture

That, at least, is the direction of all social policy, and others are asked to foot the bill for results of venereal diseases which we know how to control but refuse to do so because it would be discriminatory and mean-spirited to warn that sodomy might be dangerous to your health.

The Fall of Liberalism

Liberalism appears discredited. It appears to pander to special interests, sponsoring protective legislation on the one hand while championing public bailouts on the other. Noble or parochial, liberalism appears spent. Rarely has a hegemonic force fallen so quickly from the pinnacle of power.

Robert H. Bates, *National Review*, December 31, 1989.

But then, most of liberal social policy is dangerous to your health. Having left a trail of broken lives and broken marriages in the wake of its approval of self-indulgence and adolescent rebellion, it has debased and vulgarized our culture, while at the same time liberals continue to posture as our moral instructors, praising the "idealistic" youth of the sixties who dodged the draft, brought barbarism into fashion, and put personal hygiene into a mind-expanding Third World perspective, and criticize the "materialistic" youth of the eighties who want to make money, look after their families, and be productive members of society.

Liberals are also keen to defend the morality of what was formally considered immoral and a crime—namely, abortion, which one must suppose is yet another triumph—like dodging the draft—of idealism over selfishness. Abortion is an issue we are told, about a woman's right to control her own body. By all accounts a great many women are having trouble controlling their own bodies before they get pregnant. Once they are, the fetus—if it is a woman—has no right to control *her* own body by choosing to live if her mother decides against it. Though abortion is a "woman's issue," female fetuses have no rights at all and presumably will have none until they start taking an active part in Democratic Party caucuses. Because they have no way of defending themselves, fetuses try to pass themselves off as handicapped, and therefore subject to non-discrimination laws, but that hasn't worked in the past, and unless they commit first-degree murder, no self-respecting liberal would consider delaying their execution by their mothers—though, consolingly, the liberal might himself be *personally* opposed to abortion.

And it is indeed passing strange that liberals who find themselves personally opposed to abortion are humble enough not to seek to impose their personal anti-abortion morality on others, while at the same time they have no problem enforcing their *personal* readings of the Constitution on the public, no matter how little that reading had to do with the original intent of the framers of the Constitution or what the Constitution actually says. This dichotomy doesn't bother liberals because they don't let it bother them. Liberalism doesn't have to make sense. It just has to be progressive. But where exactly is it progressing to, no one knows, except that it is always pointed left. Liberalism is no longer—if it ever was—the party of reason, it is the party of revelation. Unfortunately, Jesse Jackson is its prophet.

A Lack of Reason

This is both good news and bad news for conservatives. It is good news insofar as conservatives can make an issue of liberal irrationality and appeal to the residual common sense of the electorate. It is bad news in that it means that liberal institutions are in the hands of people with whom reasoned discussion is impossible. This is why liberals respond to conservative criticism not with rational arguments but with epithets—*racist, sexist, elitist, McCarthyist*, and so on. It is also why liberal institutions are so intolerant. If they cannot understand what they themselves believe, how can they possibly understand other viewpoints? Thus the liberal is left with but one method of promoting his ideology, which is coercion—his *raison* to support public education, economic intervention, and social programs that enshrine and defend his interest groups. Opposed to liberty, excellence, and law at home and accommodating to our enemies abroad, there comes a point when one must be held morally culpable for one's liberalism. Conservatives should start encouraging the electorate to take an accounting as soon as possible.

140

*"Populism is a belief in decentralization of
. . . power. It is fundamentally a trust in people. "*

Populism Is a Strong Political Force in America

Jim Hightower, interviewed by *Dollars & Sense*

Founded in the 1870s to represent the interests of farmers, populism today has been resurrected to represent the interests of common people through local cooperatives and other grassroots groups. In the following viewpoint, Jim Hightower, Texas agricultural commissioner and a leading populist, describes today's populist movement. He believes populism can help Americans unite to solve their economic and social problems without government involvement. The viewpoint is excerpted from an interview with Hightower by the socialist journal *Dollars & Sense.*

As you read, consider the following questions:

1. Why does Hightower believe many Northeasterners dislike populism?
2. How does populism differ from liberalism and socialism, according to the author?
3. Populism has traditionally been popular in farm states. Why does Hightower believe that the new populism can appeal to Americans in nonagricultural states?

Excerpted and reprinted, with permission, from "Bringing Back Populism" by Jim Hightower, interviewed by *Dollars & Sense*, January/February 1990. *Dollars & Sense* is a progressive monthly economics magazine. First-year subscriptions are available for $14.95 from the office at One Summer St., Somerville, MA 02143.

DOLLARS & SENSE: How do you define populism?

JIM HIGHTOWER: Populism is a belief in decentralization of economic and political power. It is fundamentally a trust in people. If you give people a chance and the tools to manage their own destiny, they will pick up those tools and put them to work.

Populism has a negative connotation, particularly in the Northeast. This is largely because of historians who misinterpreted and misstated the true populist movement. These historians focused on the 1920s and 1930s when previously populist leaders had degenerated into demagogues, anti-Semites, xenophobes, and racists. The true populist movement was the Farmers Alliance created in the 1870s. The alliance was anti-racial, had labor participating in it, and had its own bank. But the central bankers, primarily New York bankers, were able to bust that bank about 1900 and that killed the populist movement. . . .

Could you go into more detail on the populist economic vision and how you have used it in your work in Texas?

Populists take a structural approach to economic problems. We had a case of black farmers outside of Houston producing watermelons. Because of the rise of supermarket concentration in that city—the mom-and-pop outlets had been displaced by Kroger's and some other major chains—the farmers were unable to market their watermelons in Houston. These farmers were seeing about 60% of their melon crop rot in the fields. They were selling out of pick-up trucks on the side of the road and getting a penny a pound for their melons.

Helping People Prosper

There's a couple of ways of looking at this. A traditional liberal approach would be to apply regulatory or anti-trust power to deal with Kroger's. Another traditional liberal approach would be supplemental income payments to those farmers. A populist approach is to change the market structure so that these productive, enterprising people don't have their melons rot in the fields. That's what we did. We went to Kroger's and said we'd help reorganize the local marketing system so that Kroger's could buy locally instead of nationally or internationally. And in exchange for doing that, not only would Kroger's get a better quality and cheaper product, but we would promote Kroger's willingness to be a citizen of Texas by buying here as well as selling here.

Kroger's bought every melon that that co-op produced that year—5,000 pounds of watermelon—at a negotiated price of 7 1/4 cents a pound. The farmers had about a 164% increase in their income. Consumers paid $1.75 for the Texas melon instead of $3.50 for the Florida melon they had been buying. Kroger's made more profit and got more publicity than it had ever thought possible and now buys other products from those farmers. Today we have many more co-ops around the state and other farmers have seen the advantage of local and regional marketing.

A Constructive Ideology

Progressive populism starts from the simple premise that too few people in America control too much of the money and power, and they are using it against the interests of the vast majority. The progressive populism we espouse is inclusive, not divisive. We try to change the frustration, anger, and alienation that Americans rightfully feel—because most of them are being taken advantage of by the system the way it is presently structured—and we try to channel that in a constructive way, to resolve the problems.

Lane Evans, *Utne Reader*, March/April 1989.

What are the other ways a populist agenda differs from a liberal agenda?
The most fundamental one is in changing structures. As Jesse Jackson said, for example, teenage mothers on welfare in urban slums don't particularly want food stamps and welfare payments: They would prefer the educational opportunity and the training opportunity and the day-care opportunity and the prenatal-care opportunity and the Head Start opportunity to have their own life and a personal economics that is in their hands rather than in some bureaucracy somewhere. So, to the degree possible, the approach that we take when people are falling between the cracks of the economic system is to fill in the cracks so that nobody is falling through rather than extending welfare benefits.

Decentralization Is the Key

How do you differentiate populism from socialism?
Socialism tends to concentrate power and results in bureaucracies that are as aloof and insensitive as corporate bureaucracies. From what I know of reading socialist thought, that is not the intention of the seminal thinkers of socialism. But it has too often been the implication.

I believe in decentralization. I begin with decentralization organized around markets, but I recognize that there are holes that need to be filled, just as some socialist economies are now realizing that there are holes that they need to fill by reaching out to the market. My basic contention is that no system works, and I'm too impatient and maybe not smart enough to spend much time worrying about the intellectual integrity of the system. I want to do what works. . . .

What is the role of government in populism?

I believe in a very activist government, but it is an activist government that is doing what needs to be done rather than becoming a bureaucratic barrier as so much of our government nationally, locally, and in the states is these days. For example, the role of the government for the watermelon co-op was not to go out with bushel basketfulls of money to the farmers, it was to be a catalyst and a packager. Those farmers didn't know who to go see at Kroger's. And if they didn't know who to go see, they wouldn't have gotten in the door. But we as a state agency can get in the door of the Kroger's and can use our good offices to help organize a cooperative as we did with the watermelon producers. We can help direct the farmers to pools of capital that give them the financial capability they need. It is a very activist role for government but it is not a welfare role.

A Broad Appeal

Populism is identified with the farm states: Can it appeal to the rest of the country?

I don't know why not. It's essentially a democratic movement. You might not want to call it populism or embrace all aspects of it, but I think you are going to endorse the crux of it. While it has been farm based in the past, it can't be today, and that is not what we are doing in Texas. One of the greatest examples of populism in action was Harold Washington's mayorship in Chicago. Same principles, same decentralized effort, same focus on (access to) capital and money that we are trying to apply in Texas, he was doing in Chicago. I think the values are universal. You are talking about economic democracy, economic fairness, social justice, equal opportunity, and then finding mechanisms and language that allow you to reach people. That is going to have regional variations. I find in Texas, in the South, and when I make speeches in New York City, Los Angeles, and Boston my populist message gets a response. I don't give a damn whether people want to call it populism where they live as long as they are trying to act on those values.

"Populism has often been xenophobic, racist, nativist, anti-semitic, and paranoid. "

Populism Is a Worthless Political Ideology

George F. Will

George F. Will is a well-known conservative columnist whose editorials appear in *Newsweek* and other national newspapers and periodicals. In the following viewpoint, Will argues that the populism of the 1870s addressed the needs of America's common people and was a constructive and serious political movement. In contrast, he believes that today's new populism is shallow and meaningless, because it does not address the real concerns of Americans. Consequently, Will concludes that the new populism is an unimportant political ideology.

As you read, consider the following questions:

1. Why does Will criticize presidential candidates who call themselves populists?
2. What issues concerned the populists of the 1870s, according to the author?
3. How does Will describe today's populists?

Do you love "the people" so darn much you can hardly stand it? Are you ticked off that "the interests" are conspiring to hijack government of, by and for you-know-who? Do you think it is high time the grasping few quit grinding the faces of the many? If so, you are a populist. Populism is all the rage now, at least among the few who are courting the many. The few are presidential candidates.

Sen. Bob Kerrey has got to be a populist: his native heath is Nebraska, populism's sacred soil. Iowa's Sen. Tom Harkin is the real McCoy, a "prairie populist" like his pinup, George McGovern. Harkin, that horny-handed son of toil and of Congress (where he has toiled much of his working life) spent a day wearing work boots and gloves and blue jeans and a hard hat, stringing wire at a Los Angeles construction site. Dipping a toe into the proletariat is a familiar shtick for politicians.

Arkansas's Gov. Bill Clinton is said to be in the "Southern populist tradition" (by way of Oxford and Yale), but an aide says Clinton's is middle-class populism, "whereas Harkin is much more of a labor-capital kind of populism, and therefore much more of a class message," which certainly clears that up. Virginia's Gov. Douglas Wilder and California's former governor Jerry Brown are called populists because they are running against "Washington."

Famous Populists

No one has done that recently, other than Carter, "the populist from Plains," and Reagan, and a dozen others. Resentment of power concentrated in the East has been a theme of populists back to Wisconsin's La Follettes and to the fountain of the faith, the Great Commoner, William Jennings Bryan. He rode the populist horse to three resounding defeats at the hands of . . . the people.

For about five decades Democrats have been awkward when posing as tribunes of "the people" because Democratic presidential candidates have had such unpleasant experiences with the popular vote. Since FDR, only twice have Democrats topped 50 percent of the popular vote. LBJ, aided by tragedy and Goldwater, got 61.1 percent; Carter, aided by Watergate and OPEC, got 50.1.

"Populism" is by now another word pounded to mush by careless usage, but today's Democrats obviously think it can help them. The most successful populist of this half century was a Democrat: George Wallace. He shaped the vocabulary, and hence the agenda, of national politics. He could give today's Democratic populists a lesson in Washington-bashing. Remember his 1968 promise to toss the pointy-headed bureaucrats' briefcases into the Potomac? But today's Democrats are implausible Washington-bashers. Their party is primarily responsible for Washington's swollenness and hubris. Besides, America arguably has only one arrogant, entrenched, exploitative and corrupt governing class and Harkin is in it: Congress.

The Value of Dissent

The worst error of left-wing populism is that it attempts to short-circuit debate by advocating only what it thinks "the people" already agree on, e.g., "family values" but not racial equality. There will be no progress without dissent and debate, and—like it or not—progress, in the old-fashioned, modernist sense, is one of the values most prized within my own blue-collar family tradition.

Barbara Ehrenreich, *Tikkun*, September/October 1991.

But people who adore "the people" must be swell people, right? Not necessarily. Populism has a chip on its shoulder and self-pity in its heart. Its fuel is resentment, usually of some conspiracy directed from afar by an alien elite. Populism often has been xenophobic, racist, nativist ("The scum of creation has been dumped on us," cried Tom Watson), anti-Semitic (Mary Lease called President Cleveland "the agent of Jewish bankers and British gold") and paranoid. Still, real populism, that of the late 19th century, at least had the dignity of moral seriousness about the country's core values in an era of wrenching social change.

The issues were money and morality. The debt-laden West wanted cheap money and inflation. The lending East wanted "sound money." The West thought civic virtue was being corrupted as the speculative capitalism of soft-handed and hard-hearted men overwhelmed the honest labor of Jeffersonian yeomen. The East thought its concrete canyons of finance were incubating the future.

A Source of Ideas

A Nebraskan who was a young delegate at the Populist Party's 1892 convention later said that Nebraska was then only nominally owned by its settlers, most of them Civil War veterans who got land under the Homestead Act. "Actually, Nebraska was owned by the big insurance companies of the East and by the railroads that traversed the country between Kansas and South Dakota." They owned all three branches of the state government" lock, stock and barrel." They raised rates with impunity and dodged liability for their negligence. The Union Pacific alone had been given 4,845,977 acres of Nebraska—one tenth of the state including every other section along its right of way for 24 miles on each side of the track. The insurance companies held mortgages. Between 1889 and 1893 11,000 farm mortgages were foreclosed in Kansas alone.

The Populist Party was the most successful third party in American history. It sowed the political system with people and ideas. That young Nebraska delegate of 1892 persevered in politics and 40 years later was floor manager for FDR at the 1932 convention that nominated FDR for president. Other than free coinage of silver and nationalization of the railroads, most of the Populist Party's program (railroad and grain elevator regulation, initiative and referendum, popular election of senators, federal income tax, women's suffrage) became law.

Then and Now

And what do today's ersatz populists advocate to ennoble the nation? Tax breaks for the middle class.

The Populist Party's 1892 platform said: "Corruption dominates the ballot box, the legislatures, the Congress, and touches even the ermine of the bench . . . The urban workmen are denied the right to organize for self-protection, imported pauperized labor beats down their wages, a hireling standing army is established to shoot them down . . . From the same prolific womb of governmental injustices we breed the two great classes—tramps and millionaires." The language was overheated, but at least it was heated by honest passions stirred by huge problems.

Today, if your thinking is shallow, your passions are synthetic and your vocabulary is stunted, your idea of trenchant social criticism will be to shout "Bullshit!" and ridicule the names George Herbert Walker Bush and J. Danforth Quayle. . . . In 1968 George Wallace said, "Hell, we got too much dignity in government." He should be happier now.

> *"The Greens are presenting a new vision and new applications of the values taught by all the great religions."*

The Environmental Movement Is a Strong Political Force

Elizabeth Cattell Bronson

The Green movement began twenty years ago with a small group of Americans concerned about pollution and other environmental problems. The movement gained in power and size, and today environmental activists are forming local political parties. In the following viewpoint, Elizabeth Cattell Bronson states that the Green movement is concerned with social justice issues that affect all Americans. Bronson concludes that because of this, the movement has the potential of becoming a strong political force in America. Bronson is a retired psychotherapist and the leader of a Green group in Bethlehem, Pennsylvania.

As you read, consider the following questions:

1. What outdated ideas does Bronson believe the world must discard?
2. What does the author believe the Green movement can offer America?
3. Why is it important that the Greens emphasize both politics and spirituality, according to the author?

Elizabeth Cattell Bronson, "The Green Movement," *Friends Journal*, March 1991. Reprinted with permission.

Today, in the most highly developed nations, we are at a crisis point, which is requiring us to discard outdated paradigms. One such example is that security can be based on military power, when in the nuclear age security requires collective security and the abolition of war. (And yet we are still stockpiling nuclear bombs!) Another outdated model is that industrial expansion is an unquestionable goal, when our industries, including our military-industrial complex, are polluting air, earth, and water, depleting the ozone layer, and using up unrenewable resources. The former head of the United Nations Environment Programme warned that the ecological damage we are causing could be more dangerous than a nuclear holocaust. Another outdated paradigm is that in our democratic capitalism, wealth will "trickle down" to the poor. Actually, the gap between wealth and poverty is growing, not only in the Third World, where it is overwhelming, but in the United States, where one half of one percent (millionaires and billionaires) are said to own more than 90 percent of our population. In New York City, the "financial capital of the world," there are 90,000 homeless and unemployed. Another outdated belief is that acquisition of money and possessions can provide a happy and worthwhile life. Psychologist Paul Wachtel points out in *The Poverty of Affluence*, all the rich know to do with their money is buy more and more. As Thoreau said, "We are as rich as our ability to do without things."

Recently in the United States, which considers itself to be the number one nation, there has been a degradation of life evident in the increase of child neglect and child abuse, drug addiction, gambling, pornography, crime, and suicides (including millionaires and children under ten). John Kenneth Galbraith labels our wealthy, "affluent slaves." And murder is said to be the fastest growing cause of death in the country. When the old is breaking down, there needs to be the emergence of new possibilities, and a transformative perception. This is what the Green movement is offering.

The History of the Greens

The Green movement started in Europe in the late 1970s, and made the headlines in March 1983 when, in West Germany, 27 people carrying a globe and the branch of a tree from the Black Forest, which was dying of pollution, entered the Bundestag as the first new party to be elected in more than 30 years. "Die Grünen" is founded on four pillars: ecological sustainability, social responsibility, grassroots democracy, and nonviolence. The Green movement has spread to many countries, including Belgium, France, Sweden, Austria, England, Ireland, Finland, East Germany, Spain, Greece, Portugal, Canada, the United States, Japan, the Soviet Union, and the Philippines. More recently, Green groups have started in Argentina, Brazil, and Australia.

In the United States, a group gathered in St. Paul, Minnesota, August 1984, to formally establish a U.S. Green movement. They founded the Green Committees of Correspondence (GCoC) "to provide a focal point for local and autonomous Green groups," and have opened a clearing house in Kansas City, Missouri, which some describe as "a lamp to provide a new, creative vision, that will take us to a fuller, deeper way of life." The first national conference was held in Amherst, Massachusetts, July 1987, at which Charlene Spretnak urged that Green programs contain spirituality as a priority value. The Greens hold local meetings, regional meetings, and yearly meetings bringing together Greens from all over the country and beyond. Ideas and concerns are shared, not imposed, and decisions are made through consensus.

An Alternative Political Voice

Green activists in the U.S. have established an impressive, though not widely noticed, record of grass-roots successes around local environmental issues. At the same time, Greens have been slowly building support for a political outlook that merges ecological and social activism, with a strong emphasis on participatory democracy and political and economic decentralization. The Greens have helped sustain a hopeful alternative voice in a period characterized by a distinct shortage of idealism on the left.

Brian Tokar, *Z Magazine*, October 1991.

The U.S. Green movement is committed to Ten Key Values, which are largely formulated in questions. (Sometimes there are as many as six to one issue, but because space is limited, I'll mainly give the first question for each.)

1. *Ecological Wisdom*: How can we operate human societies with the understanding that we are part of nature, not on top of it?

2. *Grassroots Democracy*: How can we develop systems that allow and encourage us to control the decisions that affect our lives?

3. *Personal and Social Responsibility*: How can we respond to human suffering in ways that promote dignity? . . . How can we encourage such values as simplicity and moderation?

4. *Nonviolence*: How can we, as a society, develop effective alternatives to our current patterns of violence at all levels, from the family and the street to nations and the world?

5. *Decentralization*: How can we restore power and responsi-

bility to individuals, institutions, communities, and regions?

6. *Community Based Economics*: How can we redesign our work structures to encourage employee ownership and workplace democracy?

7. *Postpatriarchal Values*: How can we replace the cultural ethics of domination and control with more cooperative ways of interacting?

8. *Respect for Diversity*: How can we honor cultural, ethnic, racial, sexual, religious, and spiritual diversity within the context of individual responsibility for all beings?

9. *Global Responsibility*: How can we reshape the world order and provide genuine assistance to people around the globe?

10. *Future Focus*: How can we encourage people to develop their own visions and move effectively toward them? . . . How can we make the quality of life, rather than open-ended economic growth, the focus of future thinking?

My husband and I had been connected with the New York Greens and the Garden State (New Jersey) Greens, but it was only after John Rensenbrink, a spokesperson for the National Greens, led a weekend workshop at Pendle Hill on Green politics that we decided to start a group in our area. John Rensenbrink stressed that "to go forward, we must move on two legs—one political and one spiritual." William Penn brought the political and spiritual together, when he set up his "holy experiment" in Pennsylvania, which became the forerunner of our nation's democracy. As with Quakerism, two of the West German Green party leaders, Petra Kelly and Rudolph Bahro, emphasized that "true commitment to Green values requires inner growth." Bahro, a former Communist, is quoted as having said, "I am interested in the forces of cultural revolution that lie in no small way in Christ, Buddha, and Lao Tzu, forces that made history. Taken realistically, mysticism, at least clear-headed mysticism, means a profound mobilization of emancipating forces in the psyche."

Accomplishments of the Greens

There are now more than 270 Green groups in the United States, and they have many different projects. A Detroit Green group, as reported in *Green Letter*, took on the goal of planting 6,000 trees. A New Hampshire group has drafted a Toxics Transition Act to phase out the use of toxics in the economy by the year 2000. Green activists met in Sacramento to launch a Green Party in California, which will fund candidates in elections. Although only some Greens are vegetarians, in the leading article in *Green Times* (Summer of 1989), a member of the North Texas Greens interviewed John Robbins, author of *Diet for a New America*, and only son of the founder of Baskin-Robbins Ice Cream Co. Out of conscience he walked away from a $20 million inheritance to try to awaken people to the fact that "the single most powerful driving force behind the devastation of the hemisphere is addiction to meat." In the United States, he says, "over four million acres of cropland are being lost to erosion every year, 85 percent of which is directly related to livestock raising." When our local group, Earthrise Greens, started, one of our founding members, Quiet Spirit, an American Indian spiritual leader, was carrying an Earth Prayer staff and leading children and adults to protest a nuclear power plant on the Delaware River. Now Earthrise Greens hopes to establish a Green Publishing Co-operative and a Spiritual Green Network to bring together people of all religions and spiritual paths to spread and implement the Ten Key Values.

Albert Einstein declared, "The problem today is not of the head, but of the heart." And E. F. Schumacher warned, "Modern civilization can survive only if it begins to educate the heart, which is the source of wisdom." The Ten Key Values of the Greens are both heartfelt and wise. As Richard Myers, previous co-ordinator of the Delaware Valley Greens says, "The Greens seek to politicize the spiritual and spiritualize politics . . . a path toward a transformative culture." The Greens are presenting a new vision and new applications of the values taught by all the great religions—compassion, love, nonviolence, responsibility, forgiveness, reverence for life.

"Unchecked, the environmental movement can mean the End of Civilization."

The Environmental Movement Threatens Humanity

Ron Arnold

Ron Arnold is the executive vice president of the Center for the Defense of Free Enterprise, a Bellevue, Washington organization that promotes strengthening free enterprise and opposes excessive environmental restrictions. In the following viewpoint, Arnold asserts that the growing environmental movement threatens not just America's economy, but also Americans themselves. Arnold contends that the ultimate goal of many environmentalists is to reduce humanity's quality of life and perhaps even to sacrifice humanity to benefit nature.

As you read, consider the following questions:

1. How does environmentalism threaten civilization, in the author's opinion?
2. What does the author mean when he describes environmentalism as the "third great wave" in Western history?
3. How should the environment be treated, in Arnold's opinion?

Excerpted from *Defending Free Enterprise: How to Raise Hell for the Wise Use of Resources* by Ron Arnold, published by the Center for the Defense of Free Enterprise, in Bellevue, WA, 1992. Reprinted with permission.

Eternal vigilance is the price of liberty.

—Attributed to Jefferson

The most dangerous ideals are not those that are false, but those that convince so thoroughly that people will do anything to attain them.

—Alston Chase

The cold war is over. Democracy won. Fledgling governments in the former Soviet bloc say goodbye to the utopian planned economies of Marx and Lenin. Hopeful new entrepreneurs slog through the wreckage of the ideological superstate, aspiring to the good common sense of the market. Tensions throughout the world ease. Free enterprise has never looked better.

Why, then, do we need an instruction manual in defending free enterprise? . . .

This is why: As Marxian socialism dissolves in the meltdown of the Soviet Empire, the vision of a new utopia is greening around the world. Like all utopias, it threatens freedom with yet another version of the totalitarian state.

The New Utopia is Nature.

But not Nature in any ordinary sense. Unspoiled, pristine, ideal Nature. Capital "N" Nature. Nature without Man. Ideal Nature evokes a revolutionary zeal equal to anything the world has ever seen.

A Threat to Civilization

Yes, the New Utopia is Nature.

And its prophet is the environmental movement.

The global back-to-nature movement constitutes an unprecedented threat to free enterprise. Overzealous environmental regulations have already fettered enterprise and damaged economies all over the world. That much nearly anyone can see. But environmentalism also poses a grave threat to civilization itself *by forbidding human access to the vital natural resources civilization needs in order to survive.* And that, very few can yet see.

I am well aware that portraying the environmental movement as a credible threat to civilization seems preposterous. On the face of it, the idea seems as absurd as Woody Allen becoming Führer of a restored Third Reich. But it is no joke to millions whose lives are being destroyed by environmentalism. Ask the thousands of Pacific Northwest logging families thrown out of work by environmental activists in the Spotted Owl campaign: they know it's true.

Ask the thousands of ranchers in the Southwest whose heritage is being destroyed by environmental activists clamoring for ruinous grazing fees: they know it's true. Ask the hundreds of thousands of workers in basic resource industries from farming to mining to manufacturing who find themselves being strangled to death by environmental activists shutting down everything: they know it's true.

Chuck Asay by permission of the *Colorado Springs Gazette-Telegraph.*

Implausible as it may seem that environmentalism poses a dire threat to civilization, some of America's greatest thinkers see it plainly. Social analyst Robert Nisbet wrote in 1982:

It is entirely possible that when the history of the twentieth century is finally written, the single most important social movement of the period will be judged to be environmentalism. Beginning early in the century as an effort by a few far-seeing individuals in America to bring about the prudent use of natural resources in the interest of extending economic growth as far into the future as possible, the environmentalist cause has become today almost a mass movement, its present objective little less than the transformation of government, economy, and society in the interest of what can only be properly called the liberation of nature from human exploitation. Environmentalism is now well on its way to becoming the third great wave of the redemptive struggle in Western history, the first being Christianity, the second modern socialism. In its way, the dream of a perfect physical environment has all the revolutionary potential that lay both in the Christian vision of mankind redeemed by Christ and in the socialist, chiefly Marxian, prophecy of mankind free from social injustice.

To transform government, economy, and society in order to liberate nature from human exploitation has potential far more revolutionary than anything the world has ever seen. The reason is that "to liberate nature from human exploitation" is a goal with an implicit ultimate consequence. It is not limited to banning chlorofluorocarbons so we can save the ozone layer, or to forbidding use of the internal combustion engine to prevent the greenhouse effect, or to shutting down Third World development to save tropical rainforests. It is not limited to the mere reform of government, economy, and society in order to make them less exploitive of nature. To liberate nature from human exploitation requires that the human *power* to exploit nature be eliminated. And that means only one thing: to eliminate human beings from nature—human extinction. The implicit step necessary to liberate nature from human exploitation is total genocide.

Voluntary Extinction

Am I exaggerating? Judge for yourself. Advocates have already organized the Voluntary Human Extinction Movement (VHMENT, pronounced "vehement") which recommends phasing out the human race. Forever. *Fortune* magazine commentator Daniel Seligman quoted a piece published in the environmentalist periodical *Wild Earth*: "If you'll give the idea a chance . . . you might agree that the extinction of *Homo sapiens* would mean survival for millions if not billions of other Earth-dwelling species." Yes, the Voluntary Human Extinction Movement is a small faction of the overall environmental movement. Yes, it is an insane idea. But these are the *moderates* in the debate over human extinction.

David M. Graber, a research biologist employed by the National Park Service—a white-hat federal agency if ever there was one—wrote in his book review of Bill McKibben's *The End of Nature* for the *Los Angeles Times*:

Human happiness, and certainly human fecundity, are not as important as a wild and healthy planet. I know social scientists who remind me that people are part of nature, but it isn't true. Somewhere along the line—at about a billion years ago—we quit the contract and became a cancer. We have become a plague upon ourselves and upon the Earth. It is cosmically unlikely that the developed world will choose to end its orgy of fossil energy consumption, and the Third World its suicidal consumption of landscape. Until such time as homo sapiens should decide to rejoin nature, some of us can only hope for the right virus to come along.

As commentator Robert G. Williscroft wrote, "it is only a short step from wishing for the right virus to creating and distributing one. It only takes a few drops of anthrax virus in the Los Angeles water system to kill the entire population of Southern California.". . . .

A Dangerous Ideal

As Alston Chase admonished in the superscription, the most dangerous ideals are not those that are false, but those that convince so thoroughly that people will do anything to attain them.

Unchecked, the environmental movement can mean the End of Civilization.

Magnified, the environmental movement can mean the End of Humanity.

Environmentalism is a very real threat. Not just to the Status Quo or to entrenched corporate interests. To everyone. To you. To your children and grandchildren. To the future of all humanity. . . .

I . . . talk a great deal about fighting against environmentalists. Never interpret that as fighting against the environment. The environment and environmentalism are two different things. The environment is our home and our workplace and the matrix of our entire existence, our physical and psychological fountainhead and destiny. It is to be treated with love and care and respect as well as with struggle, adventure and challenge. Environmentalism, on the other hand, is a particular political philosophy with a specific spectrum of beliefs, all designed to gain and wield political power. That power is used solely to damage and destroy civilization—and ultimately to destroy humanity.

An Environment Without Environmentalism

Although I advocate that we put an end to environmentalism once and for all, mine is no call for rape, scrape, and ruin. I do not justify irresponsible acts in the environment. I do not deny that humans cause serious environmental problems. I do not excuse us for causing such problems. I simply submit a warning and a message. Mine is a warning that environmentalism presents a most dangerous ideal which convinces so thoroughly that people will do anything to attain it, even destroy humanity forever. Mine is a message that it is possible to protect the environment without the political philosophy of environmentalism.

158

"When Americans say that politics has nothing to do with what really matters, they are largely right."

Political Ideologies Are Unimportant to Americans

E.J. Dionne Jr.

E.J. Dionne Jr. is the author of *Why Americans Hate Politics*, a controversial, widely acclaimed book that analyzes American politics and Americans' decreased participation in the political process. Dionne writes for the *Washington Post*. In the following viewpoint, he describes how the extremes of liberalism in the 1960s and conservatism in the 1980s left many middle-class Americans without a meaningful and effective political ideology. Americans must discover a new ideology in the values of citizenship and civic virtue, Dionne believes, if they are to find practical solutions to many of the problems facing the nation.

As you read, consider the following questions:

1. What does the author cite as the various virtues and flaws of the 1960s' liberalism and the 1980s' conservatism?
2. Why has the electoral process become "technocratic," as the author maintains?
3. Dionne states that today's liberalism is based on the goals of altruism and conciliation. Why does he believe that these goals are inadequate?

Is it possible for a nation to learn from thirty years of political debate? Can partisans in the debate accept that wisdom is not the exclusive province of one side of the barricades?

The Sixties Left and the Eighties Right had far more in common than either realized. If they shared a virtue, it was their mutual, if differently expressed, hope that politics could find ways of liberating the potential of individuals and fostering benevolent communities. If they shared a flaw, it was expecting far too much of politics. For both the Sixties Left and the Eighties Right, politics became the arena in which moral and ethical questions could be settled once and for all. Partisans of the Sixties Left could not understand how anyone could reject their insistence on tolerance and compassion. Partisans of the Eighties Right could not understand how anyone could reject their insistence on hard work and personal responsibility.

In both their virtues and their flaws, the Sixties Left and the Eighties Right were caught up in the tensions and ironies that have characterized politics throughout American history. As James A. Morone argued in his brilliant book *The Democratic Wish*, American politics is characterized by both "a dread and a yearning." The dread is a "fear of public power as a threat to liberty." The yearning, said Morone, a Brown University political scientist, is "an alternative faith in direct, communal democracy," the idea that Americans could "put aside their government and rule themselves directly." Put another way, Americans yearn simultaneously for untrammeled personal liberty and a strong sense of community that allows burdens and benefits to be shared fairly and willingly, apportioned through democratic decisions.

High Aspirations, Impractical Policies

In their very different ways, the Sixties Left and the Eighties Right reflected both of these honorable impulses—and all of their contradictions. The "if-it-feels-good-do-it" left rejected the imposition of conventional moral norms through force of law. The entrepreneurial right rejected the imposition of compassion through taxation and regulation. The New Left and the more conventional liberals who ran the Great Society believed that federal government could strengthen and "empower" local communities to organize themselves and act on their own behalf, sometimes by fighting City Hall and the federal government itself on the streets and in the courts. The Eighties Right also took "empowerment" seriously and sought to give individuals and local communities more say, at the expense of the federal government and bureaucrats of all kinds.

In their respective attempts to break with the drabness of bureaucratic and conventional politics, the Sixties Left and the

160

Eighties Right aspired to a higher vision of public life. The paradox of the last thirty years is that their elevated aspirations drove both left and right further and further away from the practical concerns of the broad electorate and blinded both to the challenges facing the United States at the end of the century.

Rob Rogers for the *Pittsburgh Press*. Reprinted with permission.

The moralism of the left blinded it to the legitimate sources of middle-class anger. The revolt of the middle class against a growing tax burden was not an expression of selfishness but a reaction to the difficulties of maintaining a middle-class standard of living. Anger at rising crime rates was not a covert form of racism but an expression of genuine fear that society seemed to be veering out of control. Impatience with welfare programs was sometimes the result of racial prejudice, but it was just as often a demand that certain basic rules about the value of work be made to apply to all. Those who spoke of "traditional family values" were not necessarily bigots opposed to "alternative lifestyles." As often as not, they were parents worried about how new family arrangements and shifting moral standards would affect their children. And those who complained about the inefficiency of government programs were not always antigovernment reactionaries; in many cases, the programs really did stop working and the bureaucracies really were unresponsive.

161

The right was guilty of its own misguided moralism. Feminists demanding equality for women were not selfish souls who put the children second; they were rational human beings responding to a world that had been vastly transformed, and to which they wished to make their own contribution. Gays demanding tolerance were not looking to insult the heterosexual world; they were simply asking that they not be picked on, ridiculed, and discriminated against. The right's worst blind spot was its indifference to economic inequality, an indifference that the politics of the supply side disguised brilliantly. At the heart of the supply-side vision, after all, was a view grounded in common sense: That we get less of what we tax. Supply-siders proposed cutting taxes on work, savings, and investment. But the net result of the Reagan tax program was to *increase* taxes on the work done by the vast majority in the middle; supply-side tax cuts disproportionately favored the savings and investments of the better-off. Social security payroll taxes, along with state and local taxes, kept going up. When the eighties were over, the middle class felt cheated. It had voted for tax relief, but got little of it for itself. The demand for "tax fairness" was thus not class envy or watered-down Marxism; it was simply what the middle class thought it would get when it elected Ronald Reagan.

Blind to the Real Issues

Because of the particular myopias of left and right, American politics came to be mired in a series of narrow ideological battles at a time when much larger issues were at stake. While Americans battled over the Religious Right, Japanese and German industrialists won ever larger shares of the American market. While left and right argued about racial quotas, the average take-home pay of *all* Americans stagnated. While Michael Dukakis and George Bush discussed Willie Horton and the Pledge of Allegiance, the savings and loan industry moved inexorably toward collapse. While politicians screamed at each other about the death penalty, more and more children were being born into an urban underclass whose life chances were dismal and whose members were more likely to be both the victims and perpetrators of crime. While conservatives and liberals bickered over whether the government or private enterprise was the fountainhead of efficiency, America's health system—a mishmash of public and private spending—consumed an ever larger share of the Gross National Product. While veterans of the sixties continued to debate the meaning of the Vietnam War, communism collapsed and a new world—probably *more* dangerous and certainly less predictable than the old—was born.

Thus, when Americans say that politics has nothing to do with what really matters, they are largely right.

The Sixties Left and the Eighties Right conspired in another way to wage war against public life. Both profoundly mistrusted the decisions that a democratic electorate might arrive at. The left increasingly stopped trying to make its case to the voters and instead relied on the courts to win benefits for needy and outcast groups. The right waged wholesale war on the state and argued that government was *always* the problem and *never* the solution—except when it came to the military buildup. Over time, as Martin Shefter and Benjamin Ginsberg argued, fewer and fewer questions got settled through the electoral process. Instead, political battles were fought out through court decisions, Congressional investigations, and revelations in the media. The result has been a less democratic politics in which voters feel increasingly powerless.

In the meantime, the sheer volume of money that flooded through the electoral process made it an increasingly technocratic pursuit. Democratic politics is supposed to be about making public arguments and persuading fellow citizens. Instead, it has become an elaborate insider industry in which those skilled at fund-raising, polling, media relations, and advertising have the upper hand.

Americans Believe in the Public Good

In the face of all this, Americans continued to hold with our republican forebears that there was such a thing as "the public good." Americans hate politics as it is now practiced because we have lost all sense of the public good. Over the last thirty years of political polarization, politics has stopped being a deliberative process through which people resolved disputes, found remedies and moved forward. When Americans watch politics now, in thirty-second snatches or even in more satisfactory formats like "Nightline" or "The MacNeil/Lehrer News Hour," they understand instinctively that politics these days is not about finding solutions. It is about discovering postures that offer short-term political benefits. We give the game away when we talk about "issues," not "problems." Problems are solved; issues are merely what politicians use to divide the citizenry and advance themselves.

Conservatives and liberals are suspicious of an ethic of "the public good" for very different reasons. Conservatives who dislike government see the revival of a civic politics as a way of invoking old language to justify modern big government. Liberals, fearful of too much talk about virtue and community, fear that civic talk will mean the creation of a homogeneous community. When liberals hear talk about "the common good," they often think of Jerry Falwell.

The lack of a coherent notion of the common good has been especially harmful to American liberalism. To rationalize its program, as Robert Reich has argued, liberalism has had to fall back on *altruism* and *conciliation* as its central goals. Reich notes

163

that while these are perfectly worthy objectives, they are unsatisfactory as justifications for government action in an increasingly competitive world. The goal of conciliation has collapsed into "an overwhelming preference for smoothing over rather than settling conflict," Reich argues. This, he says, "contributed to an environment in which unaccountability flourished, both at home and abroad."

The Alienation of the Majority

Politicians have given up trying to form broad voter coalitions in order to woo the great tribe of small and strident special-interest groups whose interminable rantings daily infest the media. Political alienation of the broad majority is the consequence. . . .

When politicians, in their zeal to win the backing of noisy single-issue partisans on the subject of, say, abortion, manage to blandish either the pro-lifers or the pro-choicers—and it doesn't matter which—into loud endorsement of their candidacies, they simultaneously persuade the vast majority of citizens to stay away from the polls.

This is because the majority of individual citizens are probably of at least two minds on the subject, the first being that abortion shouldn't be an acceptable alternative form of contraception; the second being that the government, by regulation of the issue, either way, will most likely complicate the matter even further, while ignoring major problems that government should be addressing. And from that reasoning emerges the conclusion that neither standard-bearer is worth a vote. Or much else, either.

George V. Higgins, *The Washington Post National Weekly Review,* May 27-June 2, 1991.

In Reich's view, the New Deal stood on a much stronger foundation. Roosevelt's claim was that individuals had a powerful stake in the public interest. The citizenry was motivated not by altruism, but by enlightened self-interest. Roosevelt was aided mightily in this endeavor, as Reich points out, by the nation's shared experience of the Depression and World War II. "The goals of reviving the economy and winning the war, and the sacrifices implied in achieving them, were well understood and widely endorsed," Reich wrote. "The public was motivated less by altruism than by its direct and palpable stake in the outcome of what were ineluctably *social* endeavors."

Mark Lilla, the thoughtful neoconservative writer, also saw civic life as central to the New Deal's popularity. The New Deal won acceptance "in no small part because Franklin Delano Roosevelt spoke to citizens, *about* citizens." The New Deal, he went on, "succeeded in capturing the American imagination because

164

it promised to be a great act of civic inclusion."

Reich and Lilla accurately capture the primary causes of our political discontent. Lost in a narrow ideological and technocratic politics, left and right alike have abandoned their obligation to speak for what Lilla calls "the civic interest."

Community Spirit Is Vital

Talk of citizenship and civic virtue sounds utopian. In fact, it is the essence of practical politics. Only by restoring our sense of common citizenship can we hope to deal with the most profound—and practical—issues before us: How to balance rights and responsibilities; how to create a welfare state that is both compassionate and conducive to the deeply held American values of self-reliance and personal accountability; how to pay for the size of government we want; how to restore dialogue and friendship among the races; how to promote strong families while respecting the rights of those who live outside traditional family structures; how to use government—notably the educational system and the state's proven capacity to promote research and development—to restore America's economic competitiveness.

Solving all these problems requires acceptance of the notions that individualism must be tempered by civic obligation and that the preservation of personal liberty is an ineluctably cooperative enterprise. These ideas lie at the heart of the popular revolt against both the Sixties Left and the Eighties Right. If there is an uneasiness about both the counterculture and the money culture, it is that both shunned the obligations of individuals toward the broader community. "Inability to commit oneself to or believe in anything that transcends one's private interests," wrote the philosopher William M. Sullivan, "leads to a weakening of commitment in family and community and to the self-absorption that is sometimes called narcissism." The alternative, says Sullivan, is a return to "the ideals of loyalty and service based on personal trust and commitment." Americans hate politics because that trust and commitment have eroded, and with them the ideals of democratic citizenship.

In the 1990s, Americans are seeking a politics that restores a sense of public enterprise and mutual obligation—knowing that without these things, the gains in individual liberty that the last three decades produced will be imperiled. With conservatives, Americans accept the idea captured in an aphorism coined by James Q. Wilson. "In the long run," Wilson declares, "the public interest depends on private virtue." Liberals are often right in seeing "structural problems," such as the changing labor market, as primary causes of social decay. But designers of social programs need to be clear about what values—and "virtues"—they are seeking to promote. Value-free social policy is a contradiction in terms.

165

Recognizing Deceptive Arguments

People who feel strongly about an issue use many techniques to persuade others to agree with them. Some of these techniques appeal to the intellect, some to the emotions. Many of them distract the reader or listener from the real issues.

A few common examples of argumentation tactics are listed below. Most of them can be used either to advance an argument in an honest, reasonable way or to deceive or distract from the real issues. It is important for a critical reader to recognize these tactics in order to rationally evaluate an author's ideas.

a. *categorical statements*—stating something in a way that implies there can be no argument or disagreement on the issue

b. *personal attack*—criticizing an opponent *personally* instead of rationally debating his or her ideas

c. *testimonial*—quoting or paraphrasing an authority or celebrity to support one's own viewpoint

d. *scare tactic*—threatening that if you don't do or believe this, something terrible will happen

e. *strawperson*—distorting or exaggerating an opponent's ideas to make one's own seem stronger

The following activity can help you sharpen your skills in recognizing deceptive reasoning. The statements below are derived from the viewpoints in this book. *Beside each one, mark the letter of the type of deceptive appeal being used. More than one type of tactic may be applicable. If you believe the statement is not any of the listed appeals, write N.*

1. Conservatives have helped change the world for the better.

2. The single most powerful driving force behind the devastation of the hemisphere is addiction to meat.

3. Today, if your thinking is shallow, your passions synthetic, and your vocabulary stunted, you are a populist.

4. Americans accept the idea captured in an aphorism coined by James Q. Wilson: "In the long run," Wilson declares, "the public interest depends on private virtue."

5. As President George Bush has said, the best anti-poverty program is a job.

6. Liberals believe that the United States will always be powerful no matter how weak it becomes in relation to its enemies.

7. The liberal position on economics is staunchly irrational.

8. Environmentalism is a very real threat to everyone. To you. To your children and grandchildren. To the future of all humanity.

9. Liberal institutions are intolerant.

10. If President Bush would open his narrow, provincial mind he would see the social ills that are visible in the streets.

11. As James A. Morone argued in his brilliant book *The Democratic Wish*, American politics is characterized by both "a dread and a yearning."

12. Liberals believe that the United States will always be wealthy no matter how much we rob from the productive to give to the unproductive.

Periodical Bibliography

The following articles have been selected to supplement the diverse views presented in this chapter.

Michael Barone and David R. Gergen	"The Right's on a Roll Around the World," *U.S. News & World Report*, February 26, 1990.
Richard Bernstein	"If They've Won, Can Conservatives Still Be Important?" *The New York Times*, January 14, 1990.
Patrick Buchanan	"Liberalism Is a Costly Failure," *Conservative Chronicle*, April 5, 1989. Available from PO Box 11297, Des Moines, IA 50340-1297.
Gary Dorrien	"Economic Democracy," *Christianity and Crisis*, September 10, 1990. Available from Subscription Dept., PO Box 6415, Syracuse, NY 13217.
Dinesh D'Souza	"What Ever Happened to Neoliberalism?" *National Review*, June 2, 1989.
Samuel Francis	"Imperial Conservatives?" *National Review*, August 4, 1989.
John Gray	"The End of History—or of Liberalism?" *National Review*, October 27, 1989.
Dan Himmelfarb	"Conservative Splits," *Commentary*, May 1988.
Marty Jezer	"The Problems and the Promise of the Bohemian Left," *Z Magazine*, November 1989.
John B. Judis	"Slurs Fly in Right's Uncivil War," *In These Times*, October 18-24, 1989.
Robert Kuttner	"The Poverty of Neoliberalism," *The American Prospect*, Summer 1990. Available from New Prospect, Inc., PO Box 7645, Princeton, NJ 08543.
Michael Novak	"Liberals and Catholics: Political Economy in Our Time," *Current*, March/April 1989.
Llewellyn H. Rockwell Jr.	"Realignment on the Right?" *Conservative Review*, May 1990. Available from 6861 Elm St., Suite 4H, McLean, VA 22101.
Jeff Rosen	"Altered States," *The New Republic*, July 1, 1991.
Fred Siegel	"What Liberals Haven't Learned and Why," *Commonweal*, January 13, 1989.
Michael Walzer, ed.	"The State of Political Theory," special section, *Dissent*, Summer 1989.
Mortimer B. Zuckerman	"Old Liberalism, New Politics," *U.S. News & World Report*, November 7, 1988.

Does the Two-Party System Effectively Represent Americans?

Chapter Preface

America's political system has nearly always been dominated by two major political parties. This two-party system, which has its roots in Alexander Hamilton's Federalist party and Thomas Jefferson's Democratic Republican party, gradually evolved into today's rivalry between Democrats and Republicans. Although other parties exist, they have always had difficulty gaining support from Americans. In the history of the United States, for example, Republican Abraham Lincoln was the only successful third party candidate for president.

Despite the past failure of third parties, some political analysts now believe the time may be right for new third parties to emerge and succeed. Whereas third parties in the past appealed to specific, narrow-interest groups such as farmers and union workers, supporters of today's third parties believe they can offer an alternative to a large segment of Americans. These analysts believe a third party would appeal especially to Americans who are disillusioned with the two-party system. Third party supporters believe that fewer Americans vote because of the inability of the Democratic and Republican parties to represent the interests of average Americans.

Whether new third parties could gain enough support to change the dominance of the Republican and Democratic parties is one issue debated in the following chapter, which discusses the merits and disadvantages of the two-party system.

"Democrats have been preparing . . . to mark out a new path that is true to both changed realities and enduring ideals."

The Democratic Party Effectively Represents Americans

Edward M. Kennedy

Edward M. Kennedy, a Democrat from Massachusetts, has been a U.S. senator since 1962. He is a member of the Senate's Armed Services, Judiciary, Labor and Human Resources, and Joint Economics committees. In the following viewpoint, Kennedy states that the Republican party has been unable to bring prosperity and equality to America. He believes that only the Democratic party has the ability and the desire to strengthen the nation's economy, to provide necessary social services to all in need, and to promote equality for all Americans.

As you read, consider the following questions:

1. What solution does Kennedy propose for solving the nation's health care crisis?
2. Why would a labor shortage threaten America's economy, according to the author?
3. How does Kennedy propose increasing the public's commitment to volunteer work?

Edward M. Kennedy, "Grabbing the Creative Initiative." Reprinted from *USA Today* magazine, July 1989, © 1989 by The Society for the Advancement of Education. Reprinted with permission.

The Republican president—and perhaps the Republican Party itself—have run out of ideas. The Administration has no agenda other than coping, no real budget, no major initiatives, and very little to say about what George Bush calls "the vision thing." In his Inaugural Address, the President told us we have more will than wallet; the more profound truth is that the Administration has more power than purpose. It holds office, but doesn't know what to do with it.

For the nation, this will bring, at best, a period of half-measures; at worst, a time of deadlock and indecision. For Democrats, it represents both a danger and an opportunity. The danger is that with it comes the temptation to do nothing except criticize, while waiting for the Bush presidency to falter. In my view, that is both wrong in principle and bad politics. We dare not forget the lesson of 1988. George Bush was supposed to be easy to beat; many assumed that being there as the alternative meant being in the White House. I hope Democrats never again fall into that trap.

A Vision for the 1990's

Our opportunity now—our responsibility—is to offer ideas, to state an agenda, to put forth a vision for the 1990's and beyond. In fact, quietly, almost unnoticed in recent years, Democrats have been preparing to do just that—to move beyond the New Deal, the New Frontier, and the Great Society—to mark out a new path that is true to both changed realities and enduring ideals. Across a range of concerns where the Bush Administration seems frozen in the ice of its own intellectual emptiness, the creative initiative will pass over to the Democratic Party—if we choose to take it.

There are ways to act within the limits of the fiscally possible, to do more without always spending more. The Republicans invoke their own deficit to excuse social inaction, which, as Sen. Daniel Patrick Moynihan (D.-N.Y.) suggests, was probably an unacknowledged, but intended, consequence of the Reagan revolution. As Democrats, we have to transcend the narrow choice between bigger deficits and lesser programs, between throwing money at problems and throwing up our hands in helpless indifference, between standing still and raising taxes—which is exactly what our opponents want us to propose so they can run yet one more campaign on the same old outworn issue.

There's another reason the other side can't and won't break the deadlock on domestic policy—because, in almost every case, the ideas that can do that will offend an interest group with entrenched influence inside the Republican Party. For example, only the accumulating pressure of an election year finally altered their adamant opposition to the idea that workers deserve advance notice before their plants are closed.

Yet, nothing seems able to move them from their stubborn adherence to a health care system which is inequitable and inefficient, but far from inexpensive. The Administration is unwilling to confront powerful constituencies in this area and seemingly unable to recognize that we don't have to accept the dated dichotomy of the past—the stale stereotype that our only possibilities are to live with the *status quo* or turn all health care over to government. Today, 37,000,000 of our fellow citizens are in families that have no medical insurance, and most of them are working families.

More than Talk

All across the country, there is renewed focus on the economic challenges facing America.

This is the Democratic agenda.

Unlike the Republican Party—which offers periodic pep rallies as a substitute for making America better—Democrats are united behind a strategy of economic activism for helping middle class working Americans pay their bills, support their families, and improve their lives. The Republicans offer talk. The Democrats offer action.

Democratic National Committee, *Party Lines*, April 10, 1991.

The answer—which the Administration opposes, but I am convinced the country will support—is to require private employers to provide that insurance for all their employees, limit escalating health costs, and offer a government program only for those who are both uninsured and unemployed. The annual Federal cost of implementing this idea is minimal—less than half of what we presently spend on subsidies for corporate farmers. It will cost private companies money, but I think we can make and win the case that health insurance is as basic a right as other working conditions like maximum hours and job safety.

Universities insure the health of their students, Congress insures the health of its members, and the majority of employees in the private sector work for firms that provide insurance. Why should other companies be permitted to profit from their own neglect? Why should government have to pay for what the private sector should be providing? We can secure decent medical care and establish the principle that the state of a family's health should not be determined by the size of their wealth without breaking the budget or proliferating bureaucracy. . . .

Equally sensible are day care, parental leave, and other minimum standards of decency which will contribute far more than what they cost. On every one of them, the Republican reaction is outright opposition, or half-measures designed to give minimum help to the many and minimum offense to the most influential interests.

Deeds, Not Words

For two decades, family issues have been defined to include everything from busing to the death penalty. In the years ahead, the real family issues will be concerns like health and day care and parental leave. Dealing with them will require deeds, not just words that are kinder and gentler. At stake are fundamental justice, access to economic opportunity, and a chance for every citizen to contribute to our economic future. At issue is not more government spending—although, in certain areas, some will be required—but the kind of activism which views government as a positive instrument that can exert its will when its wallet is depleted.

Not every initiative has to depend almost entirely on appropriating money. If we are to see this society whole, we don't have to view the Federal budget as the solution to every problem. We need government, but we can and have to define its role differently and more creatively. This applies with equal force to issues of economic growth—which historically is the greatest social program America has ever had. Growth in the next decade and the next generation will slow or reverse if we continue to think in traditional categories, if we continue to permit the division of America into two countries—one working and productive, the other depressed and hopeless.

There is a new shadow on the economic horizon. For the first time since World War II, America is about to enter a period of prolonged shortage of both workers and skills. The Labor Department projects a major gap in the year 2000 between the number in the workforce and the amount of work to be done. The unemployment rate could be as low as minus one percent—a statistical, if not a practical, possibility. The only way to close that gap is to widen the doors of opportunity. We face a labor shortage and a poverty surplus. We have no choice but to abolish poverty or we won't have enough workers to run the economy. In short, we no longer can afford the cycle of welfare dependency.

First, we have to stop discouraging people from taking jobs, and that means setting the minimum standards. . . . A decision to leave welfare for work means the loss of Medicaid and the added cost of child care. In Michigan, according to a recent study, 80% of those who went from welfare to work and then back again had been placed in jobs that provided no health insurance. It isn't soft-headed, but the deepest pragmatic wisdom,

174

to make it worthwhile for people to earn their own way.

Second, we can't settle for programs with good intentions. We also must make them work, so that we can prepare millions of individuals to fit the emerging shape of tomorrow's jobs. The chairman of the board of Xerox Corporation tells us that, unless we mend our ways, private industry will soon be spending $25,000,000,000 a year just to bring new employees up to the standard of high school graduates. Today, government retraining programs too often spend money without imposing accountability. The present, flawed test is how many they graduate, not how many go to work and stay there.

In 1987, we launched an effort to change that with a new initiative that counts not only the output of training programs, but the outcome in terms of trainees permanently placed in jobs. The resulting welfare savings will be shared with the states in terms of performance bonuses. The effort not only will pay for itself, it actually will make money.

It also points to another principle essential to every new social program—the return has to be measurable and real. The problem today in the public mind—and the public is right—is that, too often, the money goes out whether the results come in or not. This approach would be absurd if applied in the private sector. Would customers guarantee the local 7-Eleven that they'll pay for coffee whether they like the product or not? What they'd get is predictable—the coffee won't be ready when they are and, even if it is, it will be old and cold. It should come as no surprise when the public tells the pollsters that they would like a cup of hot coffee, but they don't want to spend a dime for another cold cup of bad Federal brew.

Conditioning programs on results is critical to building public support. I call this concept "public enterprise," a commitment to apply to government programs a basic principle of the private sector. It is time to start solving problems, as distinct from merely spending money on them.

Improving Education

Third, we have to develop new ways to improve education to ensure that the workers of the future will be as smart as the jobs of the future. Today, we are $15,000,000,000 short of math and science teachers—but we don't have that amount to spend. Instead of giving up, we've passed a proposal called "Star Schools" to link classrooms by satellite so that our best math and science teachers will be available to all our students. The cost is relatively minimal. . . .

Here, too, Pres. Bush seems uncertain. He says he wants to be the Education President, but he simply refuses to present an education budget, or even to appoint a science adviser, to marshal our scientific resources in a new national effort to catch up with the rest of the industrial world in mastering the technologies of the future.

Another initiative, which I call "Smart Start," would bring early childhood education to every pre-school child in America. The price tag is $1,000,000,000 a year. The savings, according to the Committee for Economic Development, would be $5 for every dollar we put into the program, because early childhood education has such a profound impact that it can cut future unemployment and welfare costs in half. . . .

We have to renew the call to service. We don't have to appropriate billions or threaten to take away student loans in order to pay or persuade or force individuals to give something of themselves. The Peace Corps didn't succeed because of big bucks or a big stick and neither will domestic service.

What we need is an effort, which will be relatively inexpensive, to seed the idea of public service in local agencies and in schools and universities across the country, from the early grades to graduate work. A fifth-grader could volunteer time to talk on the phone with a senior citizen in a nursing home; college students could contribute a few hours a week to a Literacy Corps teaching people burdened by a lack of basic skills. You can't tap idealism with rhetoric about a thousand points of light; you can do it with 10,000 places for public service that are launched, but not run, by the Federal government. . . .

The Party of New Ideas

The Republican Party can't live permanently off the legacy of Ronald Reagan, any more than Democrats can succeed by simply repeating Franklin Roosevelt or John Kennedy. The Republicans are succumbing to the delusion that did so much damage to Democrats in the past. They assume that old ways will continue to work, that they don't have to rethink them, that they have won and will win, if only they rerun the campaigns of the past.

Change is in the order of American politics, and ideas are the heart and soul of that change. It is time for Democrats to become the party of ideas again, to apply to a new time the words my brother spoke almost three decades ago: "As every past generation has had to disenthrall itself from an inheritance of truisms and stereotypes, so in our own time we must move on from the reassuring repetition of stale phrases to a new, difficult, but essential confrontation with reality."

"The Democratic Party . . . has mortgaged its vision and its ideals apparently for a handful of corporate cash."

The Democratic Party Does Not Effectively Represent Americans

William W. Winpisinger

America's two-party political system has been dominated by the Republican and Democratic parties for more than one hundred years. Some critics argue that this system does a poor job of representing the American people. In the following viewpoint, William W. Winpisinger agrees and asserts that the Democratic party has especially lost touch with the needs of most Americans. While the party once spoke for working-class Americans and minorities, Winpisinger believes that today it represents only the wealthy. In this sense it is identical to the Republican party, he concludes. Winpisinger is the retired president of the International Association of Machinists and the author of the book *Reclaiming Our Future: An Agenda for American Labor.*

As you read, consider the following questions:

1. How has corporate America corrupted the Democratic party, in the author's opinion?
2. What criticisms does Winpisinger make of the free market?
3. What does the Democratic party need, according to the author?

Adapted from *Reclaiming Our Future: An Agenda for American Labor* by William W. Winpisinger, edited by John Logue. Boulder, CO: Westview Press, 1989, © 1989 Westview Press. Reprinted with permission.

There was a time when Ronald Reagan was considered a right-wing extremist. By the time he left office he'd become a mainstream moderate. That didn't mean Reagan had moved to the left, but it does demonstrate that there was a massive shift to the right by U.S. opinion molders—academics, corporate chiefs, media pundits, and political party leadership at the national level. At the top, the Democrats demonstrated how far they had moved to the right by their determination to compete for the same 26 per cent of the electorate that the Republicans represent.

Someone must speak for the other 74 per cent.

Someone must speak for that half of the American electorate that has chosen to boycott the last five elections.

The Democratic Party no longer speaks for them because it has mortgaged its vision and its ideals apparently for a handful of corporate cash.

There can be no doubt that the major stockholder in both major parties is Corporate America. Through political action committees (PACs) and political contributions, Corporate America has bought the only major political party it didn't already own. In fact, I don't know what's holding up the merger that usually follows this sort of corporate acquisition.

We don't need to spend a lot of time on the Republican Party. We know what its values are: that property is more important than people, that the business of government is to make the world safe for monopolistic corporations and the rest of the *Fortune* 500, and that the Government should regulate the lives of the poor and working people but never restrict the abusive power of Corporate America.

The Party's Traditions

Twenty or thirty years ago, the Democratic Party thought of itself as the party of the New Deal and the Fair Deal, the party of Franklin Roosevelt and Harry Truman. It was the working people's party, striving for a fairer deal for all Americans regardless of race and sex, a party that tried to achieve basic economic rights for all. There are still plenty of Democrats who believe in those traditions. I'm one.

But the Party has changed. It was devastated by its Presidential defeats in the 1970s and 1980s. Those campaigns left it short of money and woefully short of ideas. Its inability to stand up to Republicans has led many Democrats to ape the Republicans. That may be right if it is restricted to areas such as fundraising, organization, candidate schools, direct-mail lists, and other tools of the political trade, but it is dead wrong if it extends to principles and ideology. It is perhaps all right to have a wealthy banking lawyer as head of the Democratic National

Committee. It is dead wrong to advocate the ideals of the banking community.

Today, we have many Democrats who think they ought to represent corporations and those perched on top of the economic pyramid. These are gentrified Democrats—dandies who chase fads, trends, and corporate PAC money. They accept the myths of Corporate America as if they were the gospel. They quarreled with Reagan only over details of his policies instead of fighting tooth and nail against the whole disastrous program. We all know Reagan's program could not have passed without their votes.

The fundamental fact of our political system today is that there is little or no difference between Democrats and Republicans when it comes to matters of economic policy. The median income of delegates to recent Democratic national conventions was just a little under the income of delegates to Republican conventions. The figures put the leadership of both major parties in the top 4 per cent of the nation's income-receivers. The capital-gains crowd is calling the shots in both camps.

Both parties continue to blab a blind and babbling faith in the free-market mythology. They do it even when events and reality force them to abandon it, as happens regularly. The Pentagon, of course, hardly operates on the principles of the free market. Nor does the oil and gas industry. It wasn't the free market that bailed out the Chrysler Corporation, and it isn't the free market that is bailing out mismanaged savings-and-loan associations. The free market doesn't set interest-rate levels in this country; the Federal Reserve and a tight little band of big bankers control the supply of money and credit and determine interest rates.

The only markets that are "free" are those for capital and labor. That means capital is always free to pull up stakes, shut down the plant, pack up its bags, transfer investments and technology overseas, and move out on us, leaving workers and whole communities stranded in the wake. The free labor market means you are free to stand in long unemployment lines.

We've had enough of the so-called free market. And we've had enough of those Democrats who join their erstwhile Republican opponents in promoting the free-market rip-off.

Union Support

Year in and year out, for as long as I can remember, the Democrats have been coming to the unions—usually after they picked the Party's national chair, the state chair, and the candidates for public office—to ask for our money, our votes, and our workers.

We've always produced, even when the going was rough. Labor has supplied the backbone and muscle the Democrats have asked for, whether the candidate was a dog, a dead horse, or a winner.

179

We've stuck by the Democratic Party through thick and thin.

All we asked in return was that the Party, its candidates, and elected officials and office holders represent at least some of our interests on some of the issues. We never asked for a 100 per cent voting record or even, in most cases, consultation prior to a vote.

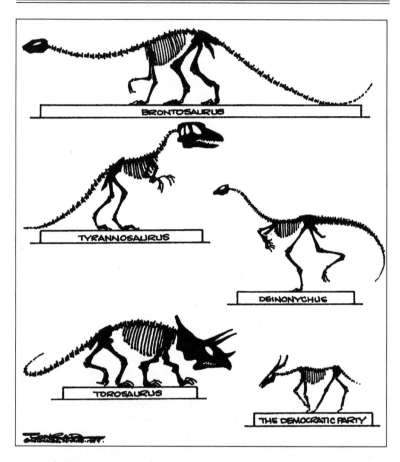

Conrad, © 1989, Los Angeles Times Syndicate. Reprinted with permission.

But we did expect that in a crunch, when an issue was up that could literally mean life or death to trade unions as viable institutions in a democratic society, when an issue was so clearly drawn that our enemies on the right and our employers presented a united axis against us, Democrats would line up on our side and give us that critical vote we sorely needed.

Former Iowa Democratic Chairman Lex Hawkins used to say, "Vote Democratic so you can live like a Republican." That appealed to many people. But, damn it, he said *live* like a Republican, not think like one, not believe like one, not vote like one.

But a funny thing started happening in the 1970s. Democrats not only dressed and lived like Republicans, they began talking like Republicans. And when the corporate PACs were unleashed in 1974 by a Democratic Congress, their conservative spots began to get bigger and bigger.

The retreat to the right, at first by slow and stubborn compromise, became a rout. Compromise became outright collusion with the corporate and monied interests that have *always* opposed the path of economic and social justice to which the Democratic Party, on paper at least, and the trade unions are committed.

The Seductiveness of Money

Even liberal Democrats have moved to embrace or be embraced by the pro-business lucre and succor. Here's the way Representative Douglas Bosco, Democrat of California, stated it for *The Wall Street Journal* in 1985, after the plant-closing bill was defeated: "Members are broadening their views about where they can get contributions, and both Republicans and Democrats sometimes feel it's worthwhile to be amenable to both sides." In other words, to hell with the merits of the issue; to hell with economic and social justice; to hell with ethics and morality. Go with the flow. Go with Big Money.

What ever happened to those candidates who took their philosophy and principles seriously and went out to preach the gospel and create the issues and lead the public-opinion polls rather than follow them? That's what the Democratic Party needs right now: leaders, not followers; principles, not public-relations posturing; feeling and reason united, not smooth-mouthed economic jargon and social gobbledygook.

The time is ripe for the Democratic Party to reassert its traditional values, regroup its coalition, and reassert its traditional populism and progressivism. It is time to do our level best to restore the Democratic Party to its role as the workers' party, as the party of the people, a party of peace and prosperity, not war and poverty.

181

"[The Republican] Party can bring back the idealism of the people—and make better public policy for a better country."

The Republican Party Effectively Represents Americans

Jerry Schenken

In the following viewpoint, Jerry Schenken argues that most Americans value the goals of the Republican party: economic growth, a strong defense, and less government involvement. Unfortunately, because the Democrats have controlled Congress for so long, these goals remain unmet, he continues. Only by supporting the Republican party can Americans regain control over the government and bring prosperity to the nation, Schenken concludes. Schenken is the chairman of the Nebraska Republican party.

As you read, consider the following questions:

1. Why do voters feel alienated, according to Schenken?
2. What is the author's opinion concerning legislative reforms such as term limits?
3. Name two steps the author believes would improve politics in America?

Jery Schenken, "G.O.P. Can Help Citizens Make a Difference," paper explicitly written for inclusion in the present volume.

The Republican Party faces a challenge—and a great opportunity—to ensure that voters know they can make a difference. The institutionalized Democratic majorities in Congress have alienated and frustrated the public. Better public discussion of the issues will clearly benefit Republicans and give the voters a clear indication they can make a difference. A recent study offers suggestions that would help citizens—and our Party—change the status quo.

There is no question that the American public's frustration with politics is high, according to a report of the Kettering Foundation. We Republicans can benefit from this because the conduct that alienates the voter is most often likely to come from the professional politicians rather than the citizen-legislator that the Founding Fathers intended.

A Voiceless Public

As the majority party in Congress, the Democrats must be held accountable for the actions that have made the American public both frustrated and angry. The public feels voiceless in a system in which elected officials pay more attention to PACs, lobbyists and the media, rather than the concerns of the citizens. Through the powers of incumbency, a Democratic majority is maintained in Congress, although the Republican message of economic growth, strong defense, and less government more accurately reflects popular beliefs. As a popular joke puts it, there is more turnover in the Supreme Soviet than in the U.S. Congress.

Findings from Kettering

The current conventional wisdom believes Americans are apathetic about politics—they simply no longer care and that civic duty in America is dead or waning seriously as people no longer desire to participate in public life. The Kettering Foundation report refutes these beliefs in its conclusion that:

Americans are not apathetic—but they do feel impotent when it comes to politics.

When people believe they can make a difference, they will become involved.

Many are proposing a series of legislative changes, including campaign finance reform, ethics codes and limitations of terms. The Kettering Report calls these proposals "either outright wrong or dangerously incomplete." Reconnecting citizens and politics will take more than legislative changes.

A New Approach Is Needed

We must take a new approach to politics. The Kettering Report suggests the following ways to change the political environment:

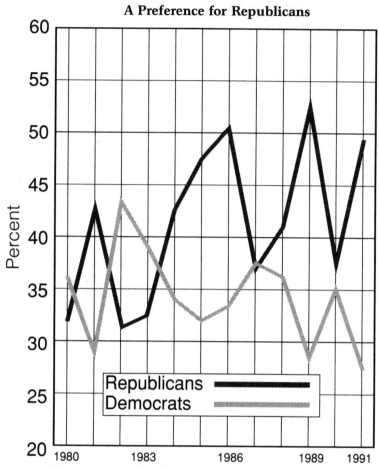

A Preference for Republicans

Results of a poll asking "Which party will do a better job of keeping the country prosperous?"

Source: Gallup Organization, American Enterprise Institute, 1991.

Find ways to refocus the political debate on policy issues and how those issues affect people's everyday lives;

Find ways for citizens to express a public voice on policy issues—as an alternative to the clamor of special interests—and for public officials to hear that public voice;

Find public places where citizens—and public officials—can consider and debate policy issues;

Find ways to encourage the media to focus on the public dimensions of policy issues;

Find ways for citizens and public officials to interact more constructively in the political process;

Find ways to tap Americans' sense of civic duty to improve our political health.

As we design our campaigns and identify and support our candidates, we need to keep the Kettering Report in mind.

A Return of Idealism

Apathy and frustration should not have to remain permanent attitudes among the public. [The Republican] Party can bring back the idealism of the people—and make better public policy for a better country.

"The Republicans . . . have turned their backs on what has made this country great."

The Republican Party Does Not Effectively Represent Americans

Steven Jonas

The ability of the Democratic and Republican parties to represent Americans has been challenged by many critics. One such critic, Steven Jonas, argues in the following viewpoint that the Republican party in particular does not understand most Americans. Jonas believes the dominance of Republican presidents since 1968 has culminated in a huge budget deficit, a resurgence in racism, and a widening gap between the rich and the poor. The party represents the wealthy, Jonas contends, and must be replaced. Jonas, the author of six books, is a professor of preventative medicine at the State University of New York in Stony Brook. He has also studied social policy at the London School of Economics.

As you read, consider the following questions:

1. How did the Republicans use the Persian Gulf War, in the author's opinion?
2. What must the Democrats do to defeat the Republicans, according to Jonas?
3. What does the author believe is the Republican agenda?

This [viewpoint] is clearly, frankly, unabashedly partisan. It holds that, while there has surely been Democratic complicity in taking the country to its present parlous condition, the primary responsibility lies with the Republican Party which has been in control of the White House for all but four of the 23 years since 1968. Congress makes law and authorizes expenditures, but it is the Administration that makes policy and determines how money is to be spent, sets the tone and provides the leadership (or lack of it), defines the national agenda. Especially detrimental to the national interest have been the years of the Reagan-Bush Administration.

This Administration has created and implemented many of the policies that have affected us so badly. This Administration has not demonstrated the inclination nor the ability to deal with the problems it created or exacerbated. The Persian Gulf War was many things, but prominent for the Bush Administration, it was a most useful diversion and distraction of the country's attention and energy from the difficulties we face right here at home. If nothing else, the War cleared the front pages of the person who had become the physical embodiment of one of the worst excesses of Republican deregulation, immorality, disrespect for the law, and greed, the President's son, Neil Bush. . . .

The Democrats Must Act

The political message to the people is that in no way can the Republican Party be expected to clean up the mess which is so significantly its creation. President Bush made that clear with the blandness, the irrelevance, and the cost-shifting nature of the proposals he made to deal with the selected list of domestic issues he chose to address immediately upon the conclusion of the Gulf War.

There is a clear message to the Democratic Party in all of this: to secure the future of our country it must take up the challenge. But it cannot do that by continuing to think elections can be won and that it can govern effectively, by looking as much as possible like the Republican Party. Democrats must be Democrats, not Republicans. They must emerge from the cozy Center-Right Coalition in Washington of which they have been a part since the mid-1970s. They must distinguish themselves from the Republicans on every issue, from taxation policy to race relations.

The Democrats must reach back to the great Democrats: Kennedy, Roosevelt, Wilson, Madison, and above all, Jefferson. They must reach back to, and once again make themselves the champions of, the true ideals of the United States of America: the values, the policies, and the life-outlook embodied in the Declaration of Independence and the Constitution. The

187

Republicans, especially in the Reagan-Bush era, on every issue from freedom of choice(s) to equality of economic opportunity have turned their backs on what has made this country great. The Democrats must return the country to its greatness. To do this, the Democrats must adopt a new campaign and electoral strategy. . . .

The Party of the Wealthy

Since Bush became president, we have had the lowest growth rate in 50 years—less than 1 percent a year. In addition, the financial system is wobbly; the schools don't educate; the infrastructure is falling apart; streets are unsafe; the traffic gets worse; we have had some of the biggest scandals in history, and a large majority of voters are convinced that the Republicans work too much to protect the rich and big business. . . . Only 11 percent see the GOP as the tribune of the middle class.

Mortimer B. Zuckerman, *U.S. News & World Report*, October 21, 1991.

Since 1968, the United States has:
• Wasted hundreds of billions of dollars buying weapons it didn't need.
• Accumulated a huge debt, with interest payments that have crippled Federal government initiative.
• Fallen from being the world's leading creditor to become the world's leading debtor.
• Ignored a rapidly growing agenda of vital, expensive, national domestic projects. Not attending to them threatens serious political, economic, and social consequences.
• Surrendered its position as the world's leading industrial economy, in terms of per capita gross national product.
• Faced a growing assault on the individual liberty and personal choice on matters of conscience that are supposed to be guaranteed to all Americans by the Bill of Rights.
• Seen a resurgence in racism and the rebirth of racial politics.
• Experienced a widening gap between rich and poor, a decline in moral values, and a celebration of the personal code: "every-man-for-himself-and-the-devil-take-the-hindmost."
In the face of these problems, the nation and its political system appear to be adrift. The Democrats in Congress today have no coherent program for treating them. In 1990 President Bush encountered rebuffs across the nation to his *volte-face* on taxes and his inability to deal with domestic challenges. He responded, not by facing those challenges at home, but by finding a new one abroad. And the foreign challenger, up to the moment he became one, had been a *de facto* ally. Using the world's

most advanced armed force, the President easily defeated an opponent which had a gross national product the size of Kentucky's, a population less than the size of New York's (of whom 45% were children under 16), and a tired Army with no effective air or sea arms, quite third-rate regardless of the prewar public relations build-up it had received in this country. Riding the crest of this military victory, the President appears to promise nothing more than a return to old-fashioned Republican politics of empty flag-waving, veiled racism, and no-more-new-taxes. Hardly a promise for meeting challenges. . . .

The Republican Agenda

With no effective political opposition to such a simplistic, distracting platform, Republicans win elections for those who stand on it. With the easy victory in the Gulf War, the Republicans will be cleaving closely to this agenda more than ever. After they have won with it, they have dealt with few real problems, met a few of the challenges sideways at best, and actually intensified many of them. The Democrats have simply failed to find the formula for effectively hammering that point home.

The Democrats have also failed to demonstrate that the agenda the Republicans present is primarily for show. The Republicans have a real agenda, of course, but they don't talk about it too openly, too often. It's a short one: favor the rich and powerful, use public funds for private aggrandizement, rape the environment for private profit, demolish trade unionism, export American jobs to increase profits, protect the oil industry at all costs, destroy community responsibility, encourage racism, restrict individual liberty. How do they get away with this patent deception? Through their own cleverness and Democratic fear and inaction.

The Republicans have wrapped themselves and their agenda in patriotism and the American flag. Partly through the use of this tactic, they have been able to effectively intimidate both the Democrats and the media. In fact, to an extent that one would believe impossible in a country with a free press the Right dominates political television, the most effective public medium available. . . .

What Should Replace Reaganism?

What should replace Reaganism and the policies of King George the Latest? Should we try to return to The New Deal? Should we try to create some pale imitation of Reaganite/Bushism which distributes the tax dollar a little more fairly? Should we buy Reaganism's basic concepts of every-man-for-himself-and-the-devil-take-the-hindmost, and a patriotism that is nothing more than empty sloganeering appealing to the basest instincts of xenophobia, jingoism, and intolerance for difference? Should we make a pastiche of some liberal nice, good, and fair programs and slogans? Should we throw together a set of programs which might (or might not) work as individual pieces but which have no underlying philosophy, no basis of polity binding them to what is truly the best about America and on which they can be successfully promoted politically?

I think none of these solutions will work. I believe that the time has come to put forth a new philosophy, a comprehensive framework for developing and implementing policies that will bring out the best in the United States and its people, that will truly provide the pathway to the completion of the American dream conceived by our forefathers 200 years ago.

We can get back on track. We can enjoy the fruits of our victory in the Cold War. We can repay the American people for the sacrifices that many of them made and many more will make in the future to pay for the Reaganite military build-up—which may or may not have won that war. Whatever the case, Reaganism has left us with many challenges to meet.

"We need a new, third-party progressive political movement to represent the needs and interests of . . . all people."

A Third Party Is Needed to Effectively Represent Americans

Bernard Sanders

Bernard Sanders has been elected to various government offices by running as a third party candidate. The former mayor of Burlington, Vermont, he is now a member of the U.S. House of Representatives. Sanders' experience has led him to believe that America needs a strong third party to challenge the Republicans and Democrats in national elections. In the following viewpoint, Sanders argues that most Americans, especially working people and minorities, are not served by the two major parties. He supports establishing a progressive party that would address the social inequities and environmental problems plaguing the United States.

As you read, consider the following questions:

1. What is the significance of America's low voter turnout, in the author's opinion?
2. Why does Sanders believe the mass media must be reformed?
3. What has happened to the nation's democratic vision, according to Sanders?

The old Democratic-Republican, tweedle-dee tweedle-dum, two-party system needs to be challenged. We need a new, third-party progressive movement to represent the needs and interests of working people, minorities, the elderly, farmers, environmentalists, peace activists and all people who believe they are not represented by status quo politics.

In Vermont we are building just such a party. I have been the Progressive Coalition Mayor of Burlington, the state's largest city since 1981. Of the 13 members on the Burlington Board of Alderpersons, four are Republicans, three are Democrats and six are Progressives. In the 1988 Vermont Congressional election (which is a statewide race, since Vermont has only one Congressional seat), I received 38 percent of the vote; the Republican candidate won with 41 percent; the Democrat received 19 percent. Progressives can achieve the same success nationally.

The need for a new, progressive political movement nationwide is overwhelmingly obvious. Despite the hundreds of millions of dollars spent by the candidates of the Democratic and Republican parties, more than half the American people no longer vote for President. In statewide elections and off-Presidential year Congressional races, the turnout is even lower. In many cities and towns around the nation, local elections are often virtually uncontested.

Low Voter Turnout

The United States has the lowest voter turnout of any industrialized nation. While there are many reasons why Americans don't vote, the main reason is that Democratic and Republican candidates have little or nothing to say to tens of millions— mostly the poor, working people and youth. Both major parties, dominated by wealthy individuals and corporate interests, are deeply out of touch with these citizens.

The two major parties not only fail to provide serious solutions to the enormous problems facing our society but, in many instances, don't even discuss the issues. Given the level of the current political debate, the interesting question is not why half the people don't vote but why half the people do.

The richest 1 percent of the population now owns more than half the nation's wealth. While we had a doubling of billionaires within two years, close to three million Americans now sleep out on the streets. What are the Republican and Democratic Parties going to do about this growing class gap and corporate domination over our political and economic life? Will they even discuss it?

In the 1988 Congressional elections nationwide, 99 percent of incumbent Representatives won re-election. What does this say about the creation of a permanent government, unaccountable to the citizenry and irremovable no matter how poor its performance? Political-action committee money and 30 second TV ads, "zingers" and "photo opportunities" are now the most significant aspects of political campaigns. Are the Democrats and Republicans interested in real democracy, citizen participation and electoral reform? Do they even care about the abysmal level of political dialogue?

Toward a Stronger Democracy

We'd have a lot healthier democracy if we had smaller, and explicitly ideological, parties in the contest. If Pat Buchanan and Richard Viguerie want to form a far-right party, so much the better. The Hydra-headed dominance of the Democratic and Republican parties needs to be severed, and people should be given a clear choice between competing visions of America.

Building a third party on the left will take time, money, and leadership. It is not an easy task. But it is a vital one—the most vital one before us.

The time for carping on the sidelines has passed. The time for being suckered by the Democrats has long since expired. It is high time for a third party.

Matthew Rothschild, *Peace & Democracy News*, Summer 1991.

The mass media, increasingly owned by a handful of huge, multinational corporations motivated solely by profits, are virtually out of control. Without radical changes in the television industry, it is probably impossible for us to have a serious debate about the major problems facing our nation and world. Is it utopian to believe that television can be used to educate, inform and entertain? Must its main function always be to sell products by constantly bombarding the airwaves with misleading ads interspersed with moronic programming? Will the Democrats and Republicans even talk about this issue?

Glaring Social Problems

The United States is one of two industrialized nations that does not guarantee health care to all of its people as a right of citizenship. Are the Democrats and Republicans capable of standing up to the medical-industrial complex and fighting for such a system? Is there any discussion within the two-party system about whether health care should serve the needs of the people rather than the profit motives of the doctors, hospitals, drug companies, insurance companies and medical equipment suppliers?

And what about acid rain, the destruction of the ozone layer, the greenhouse effect, solid waste and the collapse of family farming? And what about actually closing the deficit and reducing the national debt, issues that couldn't even be discussed by the major party candidates because of their resistance to progressive taxation and significant cuts in military spending? Or the illegal and immoral war in Nicaragua and Central America which, through bipartisan support, has killed tens of thousands of innocent people while consuming billions of the taxpayer's dollars?

The United States needs a progressive, third-party movement not only to boldly address glaring social inequities and environmental crises but to restore a democratic vision that today is being overwhelmed by the ideology of greed and vulgarity perpetuated by the Democrats and Republicans.

We in Vermont pride ourselves on our sense of independence. We try not to do what everyone else is doing just because they're doing it. In developing a strong, third-party movement in Vermont, we believe we're leading the nation in breaking the tweedle-dee, tweedle-dum stranglehold that the two old parties have on our political thoughts and actions. Join us.

"The start of any effective left politics . . . must start with a . . . new strategic approach, not just a seemingly new tactic like organizing a third party."

A Third Party Alone Would Not Effectively Represent Americans

James Weinstein

James Weinstein, historian and author, is the publisher and editor of *In These Times*, a weekly progressive newspaper. In the following viewpoint, Weinstein echoes many critics in his belief that the two-party system does not meet the needs of many Americans. He argues, however, that creating a third party is not the solution. Weinstein cites examples of third parties that failed and argues that these parties were unable to achieve clear goals and often represented narrow political interests, such as farmers or labor unions. Weinstein concludes that reformers must have a detailed, long-term strategy for change, rather than simply creating a third party.

As you read, consider the following questions:

1. What are some of the possible goals of establishing a third party, according to Weinstein?
2. The author believes that the Socialist party was one of the strongest third parties ever created. Why did it decline, in the author's opinion?

James Weinstein, "Building a Third Party: A Dead-End Strategy," *Peace & Democracy News*, Summer 1991. Reprinted with permission.

After eight years of Reagan, during which the leaders of the Democratic Party mimicked the Republicans, followed by the 1988 presidential campaign, in which none of the critical issues facing our nation were addressed, it is understandable that frustration would drive some people to think about forming a third party—or, as they see it, a second party.

For those of us who have long been active on the left, of course, the need for a second party is nothing new. Nor is it something most Americans oppose. Though few may think about changing or organizing political parties, the many who abstain from voting—low-income working people in general and especially Blacks and Hispanics—reflect an understanding that neither major party has much to offer them.

But the purpose and potential of a third party should be clear before time and resources are squandered on the attempt. Is replacing one of the existing major parties the goal? Is the aim to put external pressure on Democratic or Republican officeholders in order to get them to support all or parts of a left agenda? Or do we just want a home of our own, one in which we can espouse a correct line, have marginal—if any—influence on the course of events and be comfortable with our fellow party members?

There are a couple of vestigial third parties of this last type still around—the Socialist Labor Party and the Socialist Workers Party come to mind—but I assume that those advocating a new third party have one of the first two purposes in mind. So let's explore those.

The History of Third Parties

There have been dozens of third-party efforts in the United States, yet only one has managed to replace a major party and only one other has ever threatened to do so. The Republican party, which was organized as a third party in 1856, succeeded in replacing the Whigs, and in the process quickly became the leading American political party of the late 19th century. But two unique circumstances enabled it to succeed: the nation was profoundly divided over the issue of extending slavery into the territories, and the Whig party was in tatters even before the Republicans ran their first campaign. So, the Republicans came into being as a nascent second party, which was why they could elect Abraham Lincoln president only four years later.

After the Civil War, several parties were created by farmers—both in the West and in the South—with labor support. They came into being as the political expression of a massive social movement of small producers and workers threatened by the new power of national banks, railroads and industrial monopolies. The Greenback Party and the People's Party (Populists) were the most significant of these efforts. . . .

Both the Greenbackers and the Populists were essentially protest movements against the growing power of large capital and the increasing powerlessness of small producers and workers. They were not anti-capitalist, but simply opposed the large concentrations of capital that made it impossible for them to compete in the market on equal terms. Shut out of the major parties by political bosses who controlled the nominating processes to the benefit of "the interests," they sought only to exercise their political power for short-term and practical purposes. So as third parties they could survive only while growing rapidly, or until they gained the strength to have their demands adopted by a major party.

In contrast, the Socialist Party of America, organized in 1901, aimed at building a social and political movement capable of changing the principles upon which our society is based. For that reason its perspective was much more long-term than the predominantly agrarian parties of the late 1800s. And, indeed, the Socialist Party was to be the only third party of any significance to survive more than one or two presidential elections, even though its national vote remained minuscule.

At its height between 1912 and 1917, the Socialist Party—like the Populists before it—represented a broad social movement in the electoral arena. And the Party was much better organized than its 19th-century predecessors: in 1912 it had more than 100,000 members organized into some 5,000 locals; 323 English or foreign language daily, weekly or monthly Socialist publications were going out to about five million subscribers; and it had elected 1,200 party members to office in 340 cities and towns from coast to coast, including 79 mayors in 24 states. And in the American Federation of Labor, a third of the unions were led by Socialists.

However, while the Socialists had become a major presence in all aspects of American life, their electoral successes were mostly in municipal politics, where party labels were least important. Thus, despite his great popularity as a labor leader and inspirational speaker, Eugene V. Debs never received more than six percent of the vote in any of his five presidential campaigns (in 1912 he got 897,000 votes, more than double his vote in 1908).

Direct Primary Laws

For a few years between 1908 and 1914, it appeared that the Socialists would steadily gain electoral support with every new election. But American participation in World War I led to widespread government attacks on the party, and the formation of the Communist International in 1919 led to internal splits. By the end of 1919, the party was a shadow of its former self, and popular participation in anti-capitalist politics was at an end.

Social movements before the Progressive Era, whether populist or socialist, naturally tended to become third-party movements because party structures were tightly controlled by
bosses who ran nominating conventions for candidates on all
levels of government. With the major party structures closed to
them, new social movements had to establish their own parties
in the hope of winning enough votes to force party bosses to
open their doors. All that changed in the early 1900s, when progressive reformers won the adoption of direct primary laws in a
series of states. These new laws made political parties accessible to individuals or groups that registered in them and thereby
changed the American political landscape.

A Third Party?

What about the third-party option? There is, after all, a long and
honorable tradition of third-party politics in this country. Eugene
V. Debs, who ran for president from his cell in the Atlanta peni-
tentiary, kindled the conscience and commitment of a
generation. . . .

But in the many decades since such efforts lent a degree of credibility to the electoral process, Americans in growing numbers
have become disenchanted with the prospect of achieving meaningful change at the ballot box. That's why they stay home on
election day. During those presidential election years when I still
felt a civic obligation to cast a ballot—something like attending
church whether or not you believe—I sometimes voted for one or
another minor-party presidential candidate. . . .

But I've concluded that the nonvoters' party has a better claim to
my allegiance and represents a more effective vehicle for registering my protest. At least, by not voting, I'm not throwing my
vote away.

Erwin Knoll, *Peace & Democracy News*, Summer 1991.

From that point on, major social movements tended to find
their expression within either the Republican or Democratic
Party. Thus in this century, latter-day populists like Robert M.
LaFollette of Wisconsin were elected to the Senate as Republicans, and the movement of workers that led to the organization of the CIO [Congress of Industrial Organizations] in the
'30s identified with the Democratic Party. Similarly, the civil
rights movement of the '60s and the women's movement of '70s
and '80s, to the extent that they have been political, have
worked through the Democratic Party.

There have been several third-party presidential candidacies
since the direct primary laws went into effect, but they have not

been the expression of popular social movements in the same way that the 19th-century parties or the Socialist Party were. Generally, these campaigns have been one-shot affairs organized around a nationally known leader. . . .

The Saga of the Citizens Party

Most recently, in 1980, Barry Commoner ran for president on the Citizens Party ticket. Few Americans noticed.

The Citizens Party experience is the most relevant here. Like those who now advocate a third party, the Citizens Party organizers did not represent a broad social movement. And while Commoner would have been a good candidate in a forum where he could be heard, he was not a nationally known political figure and so could not command media attention in his own right.

Commoner's third-party effort was a result of confused and shallow thinking. No one in or out of the Citizens Party thought he could win the presidency. That being so, what was his purpose? Presumably it was to begin a process of popular political education by engaging the major parties in dialogue over issues and principles. When some people suggested that the best way to do that was to contest in the Democratic Party presidential primaries, Citizens Party organizers insisted that it was a matter of principle to be outside the two corrupt parties, and that anyway it was too expensive to run such a campaign. But these arguments have two fatal flaws: most of the Citizens Party's energy and money went into the difficult effort to get a new party on state ballots, leaving little or nothing to spend on getting a message across. And being outside the two-party system meant being excluded from the primary campaigns, which go on for six months before the two months or so of inter-party campaigning begins.

The primaries are the key point. As the Jesse Jackson campaigns indicated in '84 and '88, a left candidate can get a lot of attention in Democratic primaries. Each state that has a serious primary campaign provides an opportunity, free of charge, to participate in televised candidate debates. And with a minority of votes, delegates can be won to the national convention, where they can continue to raise issues and propose programs and get some media attention. Furthermore, running in Democratic primaries can unite the potential supporters of a left agenda who now abstain from electoral activity with the Blacks, Hispanics, women and unionists who share their views, but for practical reasons are Democrats. Such groups are much more likely to support left candidates inside the party than they are to withdraw from it to support quixotic campaigns organized by people with little or no experience in the electoral arena.

Of course, the leadership of the Democratic Party, such as it

is, would fight a movement within it tooth and nail—at least until it became too big to fight and thus politic to join. There are
those who see this latter possibility as inevitably corrupting,
and in fact there is always that danger. But the only way to remain immune from corruption is to remain irrelevant, and even
that doesn't always work. In short, real political activity must
have a built-in tension between principle and opportunity.
Those who can't handle this reality should forget about politics. . . .

Single Issues Make Weak Parties

Two things are clear. First, none of the single-issue movements
can hope to win much until the underlying priorities of our government are changed. Second, this requires a new approach to
politics in which an alternative world view is at the center of
any left movement. Coalitions around immediate issues—even
on something like the Gulf war—won't do, except as temporary
expedients. The vast amount of money and human effort that
goes into the whole range of single-issue organizing and lobby-
ing now unwittingly neutralizes itself while our rulers laugh up
their sleeves. But these resources represent a tremendous left
potential.

In short, the start of any effective left politics in this country
must start with a realization of the need for a new strategic approach, not just a seemingly new tactic like organizing a third
party.

Recognizing Statements That Are Provable

We are constantly confronted with statements and generalizations about social and moral problems. In order to think clearly about these problems, it is useful if one can make a basic distinction between statements for which evidence can be found and other statements which cannot be verified or proved because evidence is not available, or the issue is so controversial that it cannot be definitely proved.

Readers should be aware that magazines, newspapers, and other sources often contain statements of a controversial nature. The following activity is designed to allow experimentation with statements that are provable and those that are not.

The following statements are taken from the viewpoints in this chapter. Consider each statement carefully. *Mark P for any statement you believe is provable. Mark U for any statement you feel is unprovable because of the lack of evidence. Mark C for any statements you think are too controversial to be proved to everyone's satisfaction.*

If you are doing this activity as a member of a class or group, compare your answers with those of other class or group members. Be able to defend your answers. You may discover that others will come to different conclusions than you do. Listening to the reasons others present for their answers may give you valuable insights in recognizing statements that are provable.

P = provable
U = unprovable
C = too controversial

1. The leaders of both major parties are in the top 4 percent of the nation's income-receivers.
2. The Republican party controlled the White House for all but four of the twenty-three years between 1968 and 1991.
3. The main reason Americans don't vote is that Democratic and Republican candidates have little or nothing to say.
4. Congress makes laws and authorizes expenditures, but it is the president's administration that makes policy and determines how much money is to be spent.
5. Political action committee money and thirty-second TV ads are now the most significant aspects of political campaigns.
6. Without radical changes in the television industry, it is impossible for us to have a serious debate about the major problems facing our nation and world.
7. The purpose and potential of a third party should be clear before time and resources are squandered on the attempt.
8. The United States has fallen from being the world's leading creditor to being the world's leading debtor.
9. None of the single-issue movements can hope to win much until the underlying priorities of our government are changed.
10. Both parties continue to blab a blind and babbling faith in the free-market mythology.
11. The time is ripe for the Democratic party to reassert its traditional populism and progressivism.
12. In many cities and towns around the nation, local elections are often virtually uncontested.
13. The United States has the lowest voter turnout of any industrialized nation.
14. The United States is one of two industrialized nations that does not guarantee health care to all of its people as a right of citizenship.
15. No way can the Republican party be expected to clean up the mess it has created.
16. The richest 1 percent of the population now owns more than half of the nation's wealth.
17. The Democratic party was devastated by its presidential defeats in the 1970s and 1980s.
18. Since 1968, the United States has accumulated a huge debt, with interest payments that have crippled the federal government.
19. In the 1988 congressional elections nationwide, 99 percent of incumbent representatives won reelection.
20. The nation and its political system are adrift.

Periodical Bibliography

The following articles have been selected to supplement the diverse views presented in this chapter.

Fred Barnes	"Off to the Races," *The American Spectator*, October 1991.
Jimmy Breslin	"Republicans Don't See 'Struggling Americans,'" *Liberal Opinion*, August 19, 1991. Available from 108 E. Fifth St., Vinton, IA 52349.
Allan C. Brownfeld	"Can Democrats Change Course—and Reverse Their Growing Irrelevance?" *St. Croix Review*, October 1991. Available from PO Box 244, Stillwater, MN 55082.
Noemie Emery	"Race, Lies, and Democrats," *Commentary*, December 1991.
Harper's Magazine	"What's Wrong with the Democrats?" special section, January 1990.
Rick Henderson	"A Winning Ticket?" *Reason*, November 1991.
Russell Kirk	"Political Errors at the End of the Twentieth Century—Part II: Democratic Errors," *The Heritage Lectures*, May 6, 1991. Available from The Heritage Foundation, 214 Massachusetts Ave. NE, Washington, DC 20002-4999.
Thomas E. Mann	"The Democratic Opposition," *The Brookings Review*, Fall 1991.
Michael Merrill	"Why There Will Be a U.S. Labor Party by the Year 2000," *Social Policy*, Spring 1990.
Harold Meyerson	"A Party with Nothing to Say?" *Dissent*, Summer 1991.
New Politics	"The Democratic Party and the Left," special section, Summer 1989.
Norman Ornstein	"The Permanent Democratic Congress," *The Public Interest*, Summer 1990. Available from Dept. PI, PO Box 3000, Denville, NJ 07834.
Gerald M. Pomper	"The Democratic Strategy," *The World & I*, November 1991.
Matthew Rothschild	"Third Party Time?" *The Progressive*, October 1989.
Ellie Smeal	"Why I Support a New Party," *Peace & Democracy News*, Summer 1991.
James L. Sundquist	"A Victim of Divided Government," *The World & I*, March 1991.

Organizations to Contact

The editors have compiled the following list of organizations that are concerned with the issues debated in this book. All have publications or information available for interested readers. For best results, allow as much time as possible for the organizations to respond. The descriptions below are derived from materials provided by the organizations. This list was compiled upon the date of publication. Names, addresses, and phone numbers of organizations are subject to change.

American Civil Liberties Union (ACLU)
132 W. 43rd St.
New York, NY 10036
(212) 944-9800

The ACLU champions the human rights set forth in the U.S. Declaration of Independence and in the Constitution. It encourages American political leaders to work for minority rights and increased civil liberties for all Americans. The union publishes a variety of newsletters, including the periodic *Civil Liberties Report* and various research papers.

American Enterprise Institute for Public Policy Research (AEI)
1150 17th St. NW
Washington, DC 20036
(202) 862-5800

AEI is a conservative research and education organization that analyzes national and international issues, including American politics. It publishes the monthly *American Enterprise*, and various books and articles.

Brookings Institution
1775 Massachusetts Ave. NW
Washington, DC 20036
(202) 797-6000

The institution is a moderate public policy research organization that publishes materials on politics and government, economics, and foreign policy. Publications include the quarterly *Brookings Review* and various books and articles.

Cato Institute
224 Second St. SE
Washington, DC 20003
(202) 546-0200

The institute is a libertarian public policy research foundation dedicated to promoting limited government, individual political liberty, and free-market economics. It publishes the bimonthly *Policy Report* and the periodic *Cato Journal*.

Center for the Defense of Free Enterprise
12500 NE 10th Place
Bellevue, WA 98005
(206) 454-9470

The center favors governmental and environmental policies that promote free enterprise and economic progress rather than catering to the demands of the environmental movement. Because the center believes the politicalization of the environmental movement (the rise of the Green party) threatens America's future, it works to educate the public concerning the inaccuracies of the environmental movement's claims. In addition to the quarterly newsletter *Wise Use Memo*, the organization publishes numerous books.

The Center for Media and Public Affairs
2101 L St. NW, Suite 405
Washington, DC 20037
(202) 223-2942

The center is a nonprofit research organization that analyzes media coverage of social and political issues. In addition to publishing the newsletter *Media Monitor* ten times a year, the center produces monographs and books such as *Watching America: What Television Tells Us About Our Lives.*

Center for Responsive Politics
1320 19th St. NW
Washington, DC 20036
(202) 857-0044

The center was founded in 1983 to conduct research on congressional and political trends. Its special focus is on campaign contributions and spending. The center publishes numerous pamphlets, books, and articles, including the book *The Price of Admission,* which details state-by-state campaign spending of political candidates.

Committee for the Study of the American Electorate
421 New Jersey Ave. SE
Washington, DC 20003
(202) 546-3221

The committee studies the causes of and cures for the lack of voting and political participation among Americans. It has sponsored commissions, completed studies, and designed programs with the goal of encouraging Americans to participate in politics. Publications include studies such as *Creating the Opportunity: How Voting Laws Affect Voter Turnout,* articles, and speeches.

Common Cause
2030 M St. NW
Washington, DC 20036
(202) 833-1200

Common Cause was founded in 1970 by a group of individuals who desired to make government more responsive to citizens. Since then, the nonpartisan, nonprofit citizens' lobby has grown to include 270,000 members who have succeeded in helping to pass legislation curbing political corruption and excessive campaign contributions. The organization publishes the bimonthly *Common Cause Magazine,* the booklet *Citizens' Action Guide,* brochures, and pamphlets.

Communist Party of the USA
235 W. 23rd St., 7th Fl.
New York, NY 10011
(212) 989-2158

The Communist party opposes capitalism, the economic system of the United States. It supports a socialist system that it believes would benefit working and oppressed people and would eliminate disparities in wealth and equality. It publishes the newspaper *People's Weekly World*, the bimonthly *Jewish Affairs*, and the monthly *Political Affairs*.

Democratic National Committee (DNC)
430 S. Capitol St., SE
Washington, DC 20003
(202) 863-8000

The DNC is the primary national organization of the Democratic party. The party, founded in 1798 by Thomas Jefferson, is today one of America's two major parties and has millions of members. While the political beliefs of Democrats may vary widely, in general Democrats favor government involvement in social issues and government regulation of business and industry. The DNC acts as a liaison between Democratic state groups and special interest groups. It provides the public with information on the party, and sponsors the National Democratic Party Convention, held prior to every presidential election.

The Heritage Foundation
214 Massachusetts Ave. NE
Washington, DC 20002
(202) 546-4400

The Heritage Foundation is a conservative think tank dedicated to the principles of limited government, free enterprise, individual liberty, and a strong national defense. The foundation frequently publishes speeches, books, and articles on the topic of American politics. It publishes the weekly *Backgrounder*, the quarterly journal *Policy Review*, and hundreds of monographs, books, and papers on public policy issues.

Interfaith Impact for Justice and Peace
110 Maryland Ave. NE
Washington, DC 20002
Telephone: (202) 543-2800   Fax: (202) 547-8107

Interfaith Impact for Justice and Peace is a coalition of Christian, Jewish, and Muslim agencies that work together to effect political changes that reflect common religious values. Its efforts have helped pass legislation to improve child nutrition, reduce U.S. aid to El Salvador, and increase available housing for low-income families. Its publications include the quarterly magazine *Interfaith Impact* and periodical pamphlets and newsletters.

The League of Women Voters
1730 M St. NW
Washington, DC 20036
(202) 429-1965

The league is a voluntary organization of women and men who promote political responsibility through informed, active citizen participation in government. The league sponsors debates between presidential candidates and works to educate young people concerning political responsibilities. Its many publications include the book *Choosing the President* and pamphlets such as *Electoral Participation: Gateway to Democracy*.

Libertarian Party
1528 Pennsylvania Ave. SE
Washington, DC 20003
(202) 543-1988

Libertarians believe in individual freedom from government interference in all realms of life. The party opposes censorship, the draft, laws against victimless crimes such as prostitution, and government regulation of business. It supports free trade, the elimination of taxes, and private property rights. It publishes the bimonthly newsletter *Libertarian Party News*, books, and position papers.

Peace and Freedom Party
PO Box 42644
San Francisco, CA 94142
(415) 897-0328

The Peace and Freedom party is the largest left-wing electoral party in the nation. Its seventy thousand members advocate, among other things, extensive cuts in defense spending, a centrally planned economy, and the elimination of all forms of oppression and discrimination. The party publishes the monthly *Leaflets* and *Newspaper* as well as pamphlets and videotapes.

People for the American Way
2000 M St. NW, Suite 400
Washington, DC 20036
(202) 467-4999

People for the American Way is a nonprofit organization that works to preserve Americans' civil liberties and to promote citizen involvement in politics and government. In addition to its quarterly newsletter, *Forum*, the organization publishes reports such as *The Vanishing Voter and the Crisis in American Democracy* and *Democracy's Next Generation: A Study of Youth and Teachers*.

Republican National Committee (RNC)
310 First St. SE
Washington, DC 20001
(202) 662-1355

The committee acts as the central organization for the Republican party. Founded in 1856, the party in 1860 became the first and only third party to have its representative—Abraham Lincoln—elected president. Since then, the party has become one of the two major parties in American politics. Republicans generally oppose government involvement in social issues and government intervention in business. The RNC provides information to the public concerning Republican activities and goals and hosts the Republican National Convention every four years.

Socialist Party USA
516 W. 25th St., Suite 404
New York, NY 10001
(212) 691-0776

Founded in 1901, the Socialist party strives to establish a classless, nonracist, feminist, socialist society. It advocates government-financed health care and employee-governed industries. The party publishes *The Socialist* ten times a year.

Bibliography of Books

Ron Arnold — *Defending Free Enterprise: How to Raise Hell for the Wise Use of Resources.* Bellevue, WA: Center for the Defense of Free Enterprise, 1992.

Michael J. Avey — *The Demobilization of American Voters: A Comprehensive Theory of Voter Turnout.* Westport, CT: Greenwood Press, 1989.

Stephen Earl Bennett — *Apathy in America, 1960-1984: Causes and Consequences of Citizen Political Indifference.* Dobbs Ferry, NY: Transnational Publishers, Inc., 1986.

Norman Birnbaum — *The Radical Renewal: The Politics of Ideas in Modern America.* New York: Pantheon Books, 1988.

Lee Brandenburg with Andrew Lewis Shepherd — *The Captive American: How to Stop Being a Political Prisoner in Your Own Country.* San Jose, CA: Hampton Books, 1988.

Peter Brown — *Minority Party: Why the Democrats Face Defeat in 1992 and Beyond.* Washington, DC: Regnery Gateway, 1991.

M. Margaret Conway — *Political Participation in the United States.* Washington, DC: Congressional Quarterly Press, 1991.

E.J. Dionne Jr. — *Why Americans Hate Politics: The Death of the Democratic Process.* New York: Simon & Schuster, 1991.

Leslie Dunbar — *Reclaiming Liberalism.* New York: W.W. Norton, 1991.

Thomas Byrne Edsall — *Chain Reaction: The Impact of Race, Rights, and Taxes on American Politics.* New York: W.W. Norton, 1991.

Alan Ehrenhalt — *The United States of Ambition: Politicians, Power, and the Pursuit of Office.* New York: Random House, 1991.

Robert M. Entman — *Democracy Without Citizens: Media and the Decay of American Politics.* New York: Oxford University Press, 1989.

Suzanne Garment — *Scandal: The Culture of Mistrust in American Politics.* New York: Times Books, 1991.

Benjamin Ginsberg and Martin Shefter — *Politics by Other Means: The Declining Importance of Elections in America.* New York: Basic Books, 1990.

Benjamin Ginsberg and Alan Stone, eds. — *Do Elections Matter?* Armonk, NY: M.E. Sharpe, Inc., 1991.

Mary Ann Glendon — *Rights Talk: The Impoverishment of Political Discourse.* New York: The Free Press, 1991.

Doris A. Graber — *Media Power in Politics.* Washington, DC: Congressional Quarterly Press, 1990.

J. David Hoeveler Jr. — *Watch on the Right: Conservative Intellectuals in the Reagan Era.* Madison: The University of Wisconsin Press, 1991.

Orit Ichilov, ed. — *Political Socialization, Citizenship Education, and Democracy.* New York: Teachers' College Press, Columbia University, 1990.

Steven Jonas   *The New Americanism: How the Democratic Party Can Win the Presidency.* East Setauket, NY: Thomas Jefferson Press, 1992.

Steven Kelman   *Making Public Policy: A Hopeful View of American Government.* New York: Basic Books, 1987.

Christopher Lasch   *The True and Only Heaven.* New York: W.W. Norton, 1991.

Marc V. Levine et al., eds.   *The State and Democracy: Revitalizing America's Government.* New York: Routledge, Chapman & Hall, 1988.

Nancy S. Love   *Dogmas and Dreams: Political Ideologies in the Modern World.* Chatham, NJ: Chatham House Publishers, 1991.

Jarol B. Manheim   *All of the People, All the Time: Strategic Communication and American Politics.* Armonk, NY: M.E. Sharpe, Inc., 1991.

Sig Mickelson   *From Whistle Stop to Sound Bite: Four Decades of Politics and Television.* New York: Praeger, 1989.

Michael Nelson, ed.   *The Elections of 1988.* Washington, DC: Congressional Quarterly Press, 1989.

P.J. O'Rourke   *Parliament of Whores: A Lone Humorist Attempts to Explain the Entire U.S. Government.* New York: The Atlantic Monthly Press, 1991.

Kevin Phillips   *The Politics of Rich and Poor.* New York: Random House, 1991.

Frances Fox Piven and Richard Cloward   *Why Americans Don't Vote.* New York: Pantheon Books, 1988.

Samuel L. Popkin   *The Reasoning Voter: Communication and Persuasion in Presidential Campaigns.* Chicago: The University of Chicago Press, 1991.

Robert B. Reich, ed.   *The Power of Public Ideas.* Cambridge, MA: Ballinger Publishing Co., 1988.

A. James Reichley   *Elections American Style.* Washington, DC: The Brookings Institution, 1987.

Byron E. Shafer, ed.   *The End of Realignment? Interpreting American Electoral Eras.* Madison: The University of Wisconsin Press, 1991.

Barry Sussman   *What Americans Really Think: And Why Our Politicians Pay No Attention.* New York: Pantheon Books, 1988.

Joel L. Swerdlow, ed. *Media Technology and the Vote: A Source Book.* Boulder, CO: Westview Press, 1988.

Martin P. Wattenberg   *The Rise of Candidate-Centered Politics: Presidential Elections of the 1980s.* Cambridge, MA: Harvard University Press, 1991.

Daniel Yankelovich   *Coming to Public Judgment: Making Democracy Work in a Complex World.* Syracuse, NY: Syracuse University Press, 1991.

209

Index

211

214